No One Radiates Love Alone

JACLYN MARIA FOWLER

BALBOA.PRESS

A DIVISION OF HAY HOUSE

Balboa Press books may be ordered through booksellers or by contacting:

Balboa Press
A Division of Hay House
1663 Liberty Drive
Bloomington, IN 47403
www.balboapress.com
844-682-1282

Because of the dynamic nature of the Internet, any web addresses or links contained in this book may have changed since publication and may no longer be valid. The views expressed in this work are solely those of the author and do not necessarily reflect the views of the publisher, and the publisher hereby disclaims any responsibility for them.

The author of this book does not dispense medical advice or prescribe the use of any technique as a form of treatment for physical, emotional, or medical problems without the advice of a physician, either directly or indirectly. The intent of the author is only to offer information of a general nature to help you in your quest for emotional and spiritual well-being. In the event you use any of the information in this book for yourself, which is your constitutional right, the author and the publisher assume no responsibility for your actions.

Cover Design by Antonio Gabriél Martinez

Print information available on the last page.

ISBN: 978-1-9822-7046-9 (sc)
ISBN: 978-1-9822-7045-2 (hc)
ISBN: 978-1-9822-7044-5 (e)

Library of Congress Control Number: 2021912620

Balboa Press rev. date: 08/12/2021

Contents

Act V: Learning from a Past Life

Act VI: The Immensity and Almost-Eternity of Souls

Act VII: The Source of All Things

Dedication

This book is dedicated to my parents, Joanne and Jack, who blazed a trail of light for me to follow. To Katlyn and Collin who wrapped me in love and kept me grounded on this beautiful spinning globe. To my great good friend, Barb, who edited my book and made me feel normal throughout the whole experience. To Douglas who learned to ask the questions that helped me find my way home. And to all the light-workers who continue to deliver messages from the spirit world. I hope my words honor you. Thank you.

Introduction

For as long as I can remember, I have been driven to find my path. It's more of a push really. A prodding. A call from somewhere I used to know. It's something buried so deep I can't quite access it, but it's just on the tip of my tongue too. To find it, I've wandered around the world as if, through movement, I'd somehow bump into it. I traveled to the base of Pharaoh's Great Pyramid and, on the back of a camel, looked for answers across the monument-strewn sands of Giza's desert. Hoping to find spiritual clarity, I made a pilgrimage to the palace of the Dalai Lama; it sat perched on top of the world but did not offer a clear view of my path. In the birthplace of Buddha and the lands where Jesus and Muhammad walked, I searched for markers that pointed to the Divine; I went to the source of world religion to find the Source of all. When it did not offer answers, I listened to spirit whispers at the slave transport in Zanzibar, and in the slums outside Nairobi, I sat in meditative silence at Mother Teresa's orphanage. Prayers hung suspended in incense, yet my mission remained hidden in plain sight. So I wandered through the twisty, turning alleyways of Oman's Arab souk and hoped to discover what I could not quite name. I felt my beginning—some primordial scream of recognition—as I stood between the sandy beaches and crashing waves of Cape May, New Jersey; there, my pleas for answers were carried by the waves and wind and the salt-heavy air. Each place left an imprint on my soul; each delivered a clue to finding my path. But none provided the answer.

Follow your path, a voice whispers when I stop writing.

I have heard this voice before.

Just tell me where it is, I respond. I beg.

Feel your way to home, I hear. *Pay attention to the signs.*

Why is it so hard?

Because you don't listen. You don't believe, I hear in response.

There is truth in the statement.

My path, I learned, is not a physical location; so, in desperation, I turned to my fellow travelers. I met with healers and mediums, psychics and psychologists, teachers, philosophers, and poets and asked my questions. On the gulf in far-away Ras al Khaimah, I picnicked with three Emirati sisters who tiptoed at the water's edge after hiking up their long black abayas. I bumped into movie stars, stood shoulder-to-shoulder with a king, sat on a dusty street in Ethiopia with a man whose legs zig-zagged in broken angles under his torso, and cried with an orphaned baby elephant who wrapped her weathered-gray trunk around my arm. I swapped stories with a Tibetan cowboy in Old Colorado City and married a Palestinian refugee who found a permanent home in my heart. Each interaction left its trace on my soul, each a signpost on the way to my path. And as I got closer to it, I began to learn the fundamental truth of who I am.

I am a teacher, a messenger, a visitor. I am here to help.

Tell them what you know, I hear. *Write what you have experienced.*

Who will believe it? I ask.

It is for us to work on beliefs; it is your mission to write, I hear in response.

Help me? I ask.

Of course, I hear.

I already know the truth of it; I need to learn to accept it.

Before the soul incarnates into a physical body, it chooses a path, so it can focus on growth. It is a choice; no soul is compelled to take on a life. But when it does, the laboratory of physicality provides the lessons, and a soul determines the best way—not always the *easiest* way—to learn the lessons. Each soul understands what it chooses, even when the choice leads to what humans consider a bad life or a painful life or an unfulfilling life. But the type of physical existence is not the point; rather, the *lessons* are the purpose of physical incarnation, and sometimes lessons are better learned from a bad or painful or unfulfilling life. And while a human may live for eighty, ninety, even a hundred years, the lifespan of a human is miniscule compared to the infinitude of a soul. A physical incarnation is nothing more than a mini vacation of sorts from our natural state of spirit.

Write what you know, I am instructed.
No one will believe me, I respond. *I'm not sure I believe me.*
The logic will become evident. This is your mission.
Although I fight what I know must be, there is a part of me—screaming out to be heard—that absolutely believes, that absolutely recognizes the intuitive truth of what I have heard and experienced.

Because each soul is almost limitless, huge, unfathomable, we enter this world with only a tiny fraction of the soul we are. Entering a physical existence with our full souls would be impossible; the physical body could not support such immense expansion. But because of this, a fragmented soul does not have all the resources it once had, so the reasons for choosing a physical existence are obscured if not lost completely. A soul plans for the inevitability of muted memory, however, by establishing signposts to be discovered along the way. Like a scavenger hunt, we find clues in places and with people, through stories and songs and poems, in works of art, a morsel of music, the look of the ocean, the desert, the sky at sunset. We hear clues in laughter and sighs and tears of both joy and pain. We lock eyes with a stranger and know we know them. Even when we don't. All are purposeful interactions; all help us find our way.

Although only a tiny fragment of soul incarnates in physical form, some souls have a larger fragment than others. When this happens, the individual soul remembers more of the time between lives in the spirit world. Not everything, of course, but enough to make the yearning greater. Enough to feel slightly out of step, lost, maybe a little sad at not being able to satisfy the ache of the knowledge just beyond reach. Many of these souls also retain a greater link to inner guidance; their intuition is sharper, physically louder. They often *hear* their intuition. Sometimes they see holograms of other souls who have come and gone from the physical world. Ghosts, society calls them. It's not correct to believe that spirits materialize in front of souls in physical bodies; rather, those who incarnate on earth with an oversized soul fragment simply have more access to the other side. They can see the spirit world. Regardless of the size of the soul fragment, however, we all experience inner guidance or intuition in one form or another: a feeling that stops one from boarding a plane or taking another route or calling a long-absent friend, for example. Some of us choose to ignore our guidance; others tap into it. I am of the latter group.

"I am an intuitive, a seer, a medium," I proclaim loudly, no longer afraid of who I am and what I know. This book is a testament to my proclamation.

Sometimes I see images of spirit projected into what appears to be flesh and blood manifestations. Or, more accurately, I see a *projection* of a soul in flesh. These flashes of face and body last barely a moment. A fraction of a second. Just enough to mark me—at least in my mind—as different. I understood, even as a little girl, that I experienced the world differently and that the world did not take kindly to such difference. I learned this young. From a nun.

"We must all pray to Jesus," Sister told us day after day. "Did you pray to Jesus today?" she asked each of us each day.

"Yes, sister," each child answered afraid of being the one who said *no*.

When she reached me, she asked, "Did you pray to Jesus today, Jaclyn?"

"Yes, sister," I answered. Before she could walk to the desk behind me and ask the same question of the next student, I added, "he told me to pray from my heart. In my own words."

"What?" she screamed, stopping dead in her tracks.

"He told me . . ." I said in a tiny voice full of fear before sister cut me off.

"I heard what you said!" she glared at me. Sister allowed the students to mock me, laugh at me, sneer; she encouraged it really, and she sent me to the principal for good measure.

I learned that day that conversation with the spirit world is *supposed* to be one-way. Receiving a response was certainly *not* the norm; it was also something to be feared and ridiculed. So, out of fear, I hid my truth. I doubted it. I pushed myself to be left-brained. I studied, collected degrees, relied on logic, and discounted my intuition. I still doubt it despite the evidence of hundreds of interactions verified by the family and friends of the spirits I see.

One morning a few years ago, the spirit world decided to test my logic with a book about angels I had received from a friend. According to the authors, angels would send feathers or pennies as verification of miraculous intent. *Right*, I thought, rolling my eyes and closing the book.

"It better be a whole boatload of feathers," I said out loud just as my son entered the room.

"Who're you talking to, mom?"

"No one," I laughed and added; "Help me get the comforter, huh?"

When I opened the dryer door, hundreds of white feathers blew out. Hundreds of them. The air was thick with the thinnest white as they drifted and took their time to settle on the wall, the floor, me, my son. It seemed too coincidental for it *not* to be a result of my challenge.

"Impossible," I whispered.

"Cool!" Collin laughed in the rain of feathers.

As I regrouped, logic kicked in.

"It had to be from the comforter," I said to no one in particular.

It was a good argument too. Except for the fact that I'm allergic to feathers. So, the comforter was synthetic. *Synthetic.* In other words, no feathers.

Believe, I heard from somewhere deep inside me. *Believe*, the voice chuckled at how stunned I was as I surveyed the floating feathers all around me.

"Impossible," I said again as I filled three full garbage bags with the fluff. *It is possible*, I heard. *It is right in front of you.*

The day of the feathers, I stared at the proof of the possible in what I had considered impossible, and I realized that the impossible becomes possible every day. There are so many examples of the unimaginable, the too-incredible-to-believe that ultimately become believable. Once the impossible becomes plausible, members of the general population move on to characterizing other things as impossible. Consider, for example, the impossibility of airplanes in the 1910s, space travel in the 1930s, or palm-sized personal computers in the 1970s. They were all impossible ... until they weren't. Today physicists prove the unimaginable when they demonstrate how our intentions affect physical reality. Medical doctors successfully prescribe alternative treatments to what had been considered incurable, and police chiefs employ seers that solve unsolvable crimes. We confront the evidence of the possible in the impossible every day. It is our collective journey to find the possible in what we consider impossible. We do it every day.

As with most journeys, mine began with a whole bunch of questions and few answers. In the household where I grew up, whenever we asked our father for answers, his response was agonizingly predictable: *read a book,* he would say. I have been listening to that advice throughout my life, more than a half century now.

A few years back, I was feeling the need for answers, so I picked up a book about a counselor who bumped into a hypnotic technique that would become known as life-between-lives regressions. Dr. Michael Newton was not prone to thinking about the Divine; he was an agnostic at heart who believed in hypnosis as a way to get to the root of neurosis. But his path diverged, and he found himself being used in a different way. Through hypnosis, his patients were moved to a time before their human lives. Not to a past life, but to the time in between, and Dr. Newton studied these regressions for years.

When I found his book, I was living in Dubai where such talk was considered something close to blasphemy. Such a book could get you in big trouble in an authoritarian society. I was forced, therefore, to read it quietly, secretly. It resonated with me, though; it gnawed at me, and I came to believe there was a message in it for me. I knew it had something to do with kick-starting my quest to find my path. But, as with traveling and interacting with other souls, the way was not made clear in the book. Again, it was a sign, but not an answer.

After four years in the Middle East, I returned to the US and settled in Colorado, a far cry from Pennsylvania where home had always been. And eight miles away, a psychotherapist who practiced a type of hypnosis akin to the kind Dr. Newton pioneered, waited for me to find him. Neither of us were conscious that the other was coming, but there was something hidden deep that reverberated when we met. Through a series of regressions by the psychotherapist, I connected with my greater soul. And it was in his office, I finally found answers. I finally found my path. When I am part of my greater soul, it is me and not me at the same time; I am still the human *physical* me, but I have reconnected with the spiritual me as well. And, as I've learned, the point of being reconnected to the whole of my soul is to forward an important message. This message is an expression of hope guided by a group of twelve advanced spirit beings; they are the arbiters of universal vibrations. They are The Twelve.

You honor my journey by reading this book. Whether you read it as fiction or nonfiction and whether or not you question its fundamental truths, know that these are the memories of my experiences. The words are the reflection of my innermost truth, a message from my higher soul. To the best of my ability, I have recreated the images and intent of The Twelve, an advanced spirit group where my larger soul resides. In connecting the *me* of this physical incarnation with the *me* of my larger soul, my words have been infused with a joy vibration. The message contained within is a gift from across the veil.

ACT I

Journeys

23 May 2019

The world is full of magic things, patiently waiting
for our senses to grow sharper.
William Butler Yeats

The Tibetan Cowboy of Old Colorado City

Really important meetings are planned by the souls
long before the bodies see each other.
~Paolo Coelho

This is the story of a journey. My journey. The journey to find myself, and the journey to accept what I ultimately found. As with most journeys of this sort, mine played out in two main spheres. The first tracked with physical movement through the material world. I developed relationships with family and friends, animals, locations, and concepts. I traveled around the world seeking answers in the ubiquitous, and I spent time interacting in the social domains that dominate our lives: schools and shopping centers and a variety of workplaces. Movement through the material realm was, by far, the easier of the two spheres in my on-going journey although no one who knows me would say my life has been easy. Joyous, yes. But not easy.

The more difficult part of my journey—and by most accounts, the more important part—required the honest mining of my soul for hidden truths. It took me time—more than fifty years, in fact—to rediscover what I had always known and to recover what had been hidden from me by me. Once I found my truth, I worked to integrate it with the half-identity I had carefully constructed over the course of my life; in so doing,

I was able to reclaim what had always been mine. Along the way, there were signposts and messengers. Once in the middle of Old Colorado City amidst traditional western wares—cowboy hats and leather boots, blanket rolls and saddles—I met a messenger in an exotic jewel of a store that shared a sidewalk with the more traditional trade of a typical Western town. A tiny place devoted to the display and sale of Tibetan clothing and sacred items, every available space in the store was filled with all manner of the Buddha—weeping, in lotus position, laughing—as well as antiqued prayer wheels and colorful flags, "a splendid selection of olfactory needs," art and jewelry and *Om* tapestries.

My daughter and I were walking through the town on a late summer day into evening when the sky had purpled and the moon and stars were only just beginning to make themselves known. The almost-night air was cool—a bit too cool for summer; it smelled of sage and lavender and the dry heat of the Rocky Mountain West. The brilliance of the sun on that summer day had left its signature burnt on our necks and shoulders, so as evening drew near, we shivered in our new *Colorado College* sweatshirts. Katlyn and I babbled about everything and anything and nothing at all. *All was right with the world*, I thought, as we pushed open the door to the little store.

Cleverly repurposed Tibetan tingsha (tiny prayer cymbals), clinked and tinkled against each other and the closing door. More than the traditional bell that alerts owners to potential customers, the tingsha had the additional function of offering up a little prayer for those who entered the store. An auspicious way, we thought, to begin our browsing. We lingered at the racks of clothes, tried on the prayer beads and played the singing bowls. We inspected statues and took turns holding up incense for each other to smell: *vanilla, patchouli, sandalwood, jasmine.* All the while, although we tried our best to ignore him, we were aware of a shadow following us, watching our every move.

Always one rack or one display shelf away, peering through the clothes or artwork at us, was the owner: an émigré from the heights of the Himalayas living in the heart of the American west. A Tibetan cowboy, if you will. As we moved through the store, the space between us and him neither closed nor widened. Yet, the way he broke our solitude—only barely hidden as he was—unnerved us.

"Hello," I finally said, holding out my hand to him.

He took it and held onto it as he spoke. "I know you. I'm honored."

Amused by his pseudo-familiarity, I asked the obvious, "how do you know me?"

"You are light," he explained. "One foot here," he motioned to the earth; "one foot there," he held his finger up to the sky; then, he held his hands as if in prayer and touched them to his heart and to his head before returning his gaze to me.

"Thank you," I stammered.

"You are an enlightened one," he said, smiling and nodding at me.

"I wish," I answered awkwardly.

"You are," he confirmed. "Be sure of it. The path has been hard on you, daughter," he added a little sadly. "But I see your light. She does, too," he said, pointing to my daughter.

Katlyn's face lit up, "it's true."

"Trust her," the owner instructed me.

My mind checked off the many, many examples of un-enlightened behavior that I had engaged in over my life. Rather than argue with the generous nature of the man in front of me, however, I smiled my thanks.

"Follow your path," the owner instructed me; "it's hard, but it's good for you. Good for us," he said sweeping his arms on either side of him.

He exuded something special, this small-statured man from far-away Tibet. Warmth. Kindness. Compassion As he closed the physical gap between us, both Katlyn and I felt the growing glow of all three traits embracing us. Outside, the multitude of stars in the night sky overcame the lingering sunlight to brighten and sharpen and cast radiance on the feelings that sheltered us inside. *All is right with the world*, I thought for the second

3

time that evening as we—my daughter and I—finished our rounds in the little Tibetan store, refreshed and repurposed—like the tingsha on the door.

For a long time, the words of the Tibetan cowboy and the earnest, pure way he spoke them stayed with me. At my core, they were alive with energy, and I tried to understand their import to my life. After some time, however, I settled on the much-too-logical, not very spiritual explanation that the store owner had simply wanted to make a sale. I knew my explanation was a way to limit a full reckoning of my soul's truth, but despite my attempt to mute them, his words continued to simmer and swirl in my unconscious. Like the words of the Tibetan cowboy of Old Colorado City, there would be other words and other places and people. I would try to dismiss them, but they would have an impact. In the end, they led me to a little office in northern Colorado, where a psychotherapist helped me reconnect to my spirit-self through hypnosis.

The First Hypnotic Session: Meeting my Destiny

"And how would you like to proceed?" Douglas asked. "What is the best way for you to be the most comfortable to do this? Just sitting there like that? Is that good?" he asked motioning to the way I had already situated myself.

"Yeah," I answered although, to be honest, I didn't know the best way to proceed; hypnosis was fairly new to me.

"I'm wondering if I just need to count the steps?" Douglas asked. "Let's try that," he answered his own question.

Only counting the steps would significantly shorten the hypnotic process. Since I had already had three practice sessions with Douglas, he was convinced I did not need to go through the whole almost twenty-minute process to put me under. By now, my soul and psyche understood the procedure.

"Okay," I said and arranged myself shoeless and cross-legged on the gray leather couch. My eyes were closed, so everything I saw from that point on was in my mind's eye.

"So, come on up to the steps, and I'll take you to your sacred place. One. Easier. Easier. Deeper. Easier," Douglas said, starting the hypnotic count to ten. "Two."

As he performed the hypnotic procedure, I mounted steps that floated in blackness, wholly unconnected to anything physical. By the third step, a warm column of light joined me—a soothing orange-ish color, a color that changed when the situation demanded it. Sometimes the light shown more lilac-y; sometimes intensely white-ish. I knew the spirit as the Archangel Michael, and I bathed in the power and size and energy of his light. While he was featureless, fissures of light sprayed from him and might have been construed as wings. They were not. He made me feel as if he held my hand, and he guided me up the steps. My spirit guide, Willie, who had been with me throughout my life joined us on the sixth step, but he stayed only until we got to the door to the other side. Willie's role, I was made to understand, had come to an end. He had completed his mission by getting me to the door.

"Ten. Deep. Deeper. Deepest," I heard Douglas call from far away. "You're at the door to your sacred place. Open it and step through," he instructed, and I did.

When I opened the door, a blast of warm light—too much light, an eternity of light—held layers of welcome, joy, a cacophony of music, colors inexpressible, an undulating feeling of complete and total love. The light exploded through me and out through the door, meeting Michael's light and exceeding it.

"Close that door behind you," Douglas said from far away. But I didn't. I let the light out and into the physical world, hoping my friends and family would feel its warmth. But only for a few seconds.

It's time, I heard from the other side of the door, and I knew I could not remain standing between the physical world and the spiritual one for long. My place, at least for the next few hours of earth time, was in the spirit world. So, I closed the door to earth and turned my back on it towards the indescribable beauty of what lay in front of me.

"Move fully into your sacred space," Douglas instructed as if he knew.

I looked across the horizon at spirit beings. Hundreds of thousands— millions, maybe. They stood in welcome. For me. Like a warm wind, I felt the heat of their spirit touch rippling across my body. I heard their thoughts, knew their stories. They were both individual and group all at the same time, and I, too, joined the group while retaining my individuality. There was no contradiction in it.

Other sentient beings had already arrived, a few spirits let me know. *Others would follow,* they said.

In the moments of my introduction, spirit helped me understand I was one of many in a physical incarnation who had agreed to bring forth the message of human salvation. It was not a religious salvation by any means; rather, it was salvation from ourselves, from the path on which we currently found ourselves, and I had agreed to be the harbinger of the message in an incarnation thousands of years earlier. My agreement had come due. As had the agreements of others. Other incarnated entities in other mediums—art, physics, film, sports, speeches, works of charity, music, for example—would also be used to forward the message of salvation. The tool I chose in my original agreement was writing, and I had been practicing my whole life for the moment in which I found myself. I realized in the first few moments of my time in the spiritual world that I had not waited my whole life for something promised to me; rather, I had waited to fulfill a promise I had made.

Although I recognized that I stood in some kind of open-air forum, it did not look like anything I had ever seen. At least at first. The sky was a sleepy lilac-grey, and a luminescence shimmered in the space between spirit beings. Their distinctive lights blended, yet I was able to make out individuals from within the oneness. Some light beings stood on the ground as we might on earth; some floated in the air. All were lined up shoulder-to-shoulder—military-like—and, although their shapes were amorphous because of the intensity of the light that surrounded them, there was a kind of clear uniformity about the figures in union.

From out of the crowd, my father appeared. He was light, barely shaped, but I knew him as if he stood in front of me in the physical. His feeling and his subtle vibration were unmistakable. I could hear his voice as it had been in the physical, but it came as thought, not words. We had a long conversation that took place in seconds and traded images and feelings and experiences. I felt his side of our conversation just as I felt mine. Simultaneously. We were connected, merged, indistinguishable except for how I perceived him as separate. An earth habit, I guess.

"And whenever you're ready, just let me know how it would be best to proceed," Douglas interrupted.

Although I had already spent hours on the other side, Douglas had sat in silence for only a matter of minutes. It was the bending of time and the addition of simultaneity from the other side's timelessness that allowed what I conceived of as time to stretch and pull and lengthen.

It's time, I heard and laughed at how my musings had been used to redirect me.

I looked out and around the crowd, and as my eyes adjusted, a hazy recognition emerged.

I know this place, I sighed. Its familiarity found me although it had not yet fully formed into consciousness. While I stood in the spiritual realm, the planet of my original and subsequent incarnations was laid out as a backdrop. It was a small gesture of gratitude for agreeing to carry the message of salvation. After a few seconds, I whispered out loud, "I'm home."

"Tell me about home," Douglas interrupted.

"It's the first time I've been here," I explained. "It's not the place that normally I go to."

In the previous hypnotic practice sessions, Douglas had instructed me to go to my spiritual place. When I stood at the top of the floating stairway and opened the door, my spiritual space, to my surprise, was a physical space, one that I recognized, one that I had always loved in this physical incarnation as a human. In those first three hypnotic sessions, I expressed concern that my spiritual place was physical. "I know this place," I said over and over again to Douglas as if something were wrong. But in the current hypnotic session, I found myself in another physical world. It was not earth; it was home.

They have a gift for you, my father said.

His message was conveyed in something more than telepathy. I just knew, as if I were hot-wired into his being and, in fact, hot-wired into every other being that stood watching us. His thoughts were my thoughts. My thoughts expanded to be the thoughts of all other light beings. I knew without words because I knew.

"I found my dad," I told Douglas.

As my father's light reached me, I was given the opportunity to experience his human life. I chose moments, not his whole life. I purposely stayed away from the sadness that he experienced as a child. For example, I blocked the story about his little black dog that chased the family car as they moved from Pennsylvania to Baltimore. His father did not want the responsibility or cost of my father's beloved pet; I did not want to experience my father's sadness. Some of the scenes from my father's life I recognized because they included me. I saw myself growing up from his viewpoint and felt his feelings and heard his thoughts. It was the purest expression of love I had ever known. In only a few moments, however, his expression of pure love would be topped by my mother's. I only needed to wait for hers.

"My dad's soul got tangled with my mother's over many lives," I explained to Douglas. "She's not from home. But she did the most beautiful thing," I narrated.

On one level, I was experiencing life in the spiritual realm set up to look like another physical world; on another, I was fully aware that I was sitting in Douglas's office, and I was able to add other layers—other worlds—where I could have discussions with a multitude of light beings in the spiritual realm even as I narrated the most important points for Douglas. Time shifted back and forth between events. Some events happened simultaneously. So, as I narrated one scene, I pocketed others for a later discussion with Douglas. Each story was its own thing without boundaries; beginnings and ends, therefore, made little sense in the spirit world. Time did not matter; it was fluid. Timeless.

After a long conversation, my father's light ushered me into my mother's light; hers differed from my father's in intensity and color, but as with my dad, I knew her instantly. Her feelings and thoughts, her vibration were as personal as a fingerprint or a signature. I knew my mom as if we stood in physical space. She had come to tell her story.

Your father is from here, my mother gestured. *I am from another here.*

As she told her story, I highlighted it for Douglas, "She knew that her end would be bad. She knew *before*," I said meaning *before her life began*.

I heard her music and recognized it as I had not recognized it consciously when she was in the physical. She invited me to experience her life—all of it; it took just seconds of earth time. Like moving through the old film strips on a library machine, I moved from left to right in the sequence of my mother's life. When I got to the onset of her Alzheimer's, I felt the fear, the tension, the anticipation of what she knew would come—of what she always knew would come—and I felt her resignation at forging ahead. She could have taken an off-ramp, she told me; she could have chosen not to fulfill this part of her life contract. But my mother—quiet and kind, wrongly considered too naïve and soft—had *chosen* the hard route through the end of her life. She had already agreed to it when she came face-to-face with it, she told me over and over again.

It was my choice, she said; *it was always my choice.*

"When she was lost in the Alzheimer's, she was okay. She knew why. She couldn't tell us; [by the time she understood], she was unable to express it. Only the beginning was bad because she knew where her life was heading. She's showing me," I told Douglas.

I experienced Alzheimer's; I felt what it was like to be locked inside a dense, physical shell while still expressing as a full, vibrant soul. Oddly, my mother was not resentful; instead, she was complete, accepting.

It was just another step, she explained; *our light gets trapped in our human bodies throughout our physical incarnations.*

"It was her way of moving to my dad's soul group," I narrated for Douglas.

10

Everything is love, my mother explained. *But some souls are tied together. Bound. We feel incomplete without each other,* she said trying to help me understand.

I knew as she said it that *incomplete* was an earth-bound word, not a word that could adequately explain her situation.

It is not desire or need, she explained, and I knew what she meant even if I could not explain it. *It is a sense of completeness. We progress faster together than separately.*

As I finished reliving her earth story, she stood in front of me, radiant.

And now I am here, she said.

The light beings roused as one in celebration of my mother, of her brave decision to live as she did. Because of her life choices, she was accepted into a higher soul group. My father's soul group. In a place different from the one she had once belonged.

"And his soul group is—I don't know how to explain—celebrating her. Clapping," I told Douglas. "They're just light, but she's accepted fully. I needed to know that."

Sometimes the meek, I heard from the group, *have more strength. It's just quieter.*

My dad let me feel his smile and, while he was all light, I understood that he was shaking his head and smirking as he might have in the physical.

"She wasn't at his level, but she is now," I continued to narrate for Douglas although I was already far ahead of the story. "And the group is letting me know that she sacrificed for it, but she knew from the beginning," I made clear to him. "And he left earlier . . . yeah . . . he left earlier because he wanted to help her transition to a new . . . not just group . . . but a new place. It's new. Everything. She left everything behind. But she can visit," I explained to Douglas and, then, followed up with a caveat. "It's not as easy to visit as the books make it seem. Between soul groups. They have a job to do; they have a mission."

"What prompted her to do that?" Douglas asked.

"Everything is love," I answered immediately. "Everything. Every feeling. Every thought. Every gesture. Everything," I told Douglas. "But sometimes there's almost a bind between souls, a bind so strong that even in the perfect—the perfect moments of who we are—there's a feeling of— not *longing* because that's a human emotion and not *need* because that's human—but a *compatibility* that makes both souls better. They move quicker together. They move quicker through their learning, through their mission. And knowing their story was my gift for agreeing to forward the message of salvation."

As I experienced my mother's life, I felt and, then, saw a lilac light crackle and burn in the sky. The Twelve—the creators and heralds of vibration— had arrived, but they had not yet made themselves fully known. I understood I had to experience them in bite-sized chunks until they could manifest completely. As a physical being, I was not strong enough to take them all at once. At least in the beginning.

"My father's spirit was sent to push me. To toughen me up," I told Douglas as I waited for the emergence of The Twelve.

"You mean through your childhood?" Douglas asked.

"And through adulthood. I'm trying to think of the words to say this without it sounding too human, but . . . " I said and, then, trailed off to mark the entrance of The Twelve. "They're here."

Your group of twelve is here?"

"They're coming."

"Okay," Douglas said and waited.

"They're here, but they haven't presented themselves yet. But they're telling me they're here," I said.

There was a palpable change in the ethers of the spiritual realm. An excitement ran through it. There is not so much a hierarchy on the other side as there is a recognition of advancement by some beings. Admiration, I suppose, is a close enough earth word. All beings—all souls—will reach ascension eventually, but for those who have already ascended, there is a certain respect. I felt a tingling at the top of my head and butterflies in my stomach; the feelings were generated by the group and transmitted not so much *to* me, but *through* me. It was an electrical impulse that charged the very atmosphere and everything in it.

"This is going to come out the wrong way because I don't have the words to explain it, but they have a high vibration," I told Douglas about The Twelve. "And I'm not from this planet—earth—although I've grown to love it. I love the beauty. I love dogs," I added. "So I only brought a part of my soul here—a small part—because when your whole being is radiating joy, it doesn't always translate into human existence. And too much joy attracts the dark. Too much light attracts the dark. But it could also prevent me from finding my mission."

What I was trying to explain to Douglas was the fact that an unusually small part of my greater soul entered my earthly existence. Too much soul would have prevented me from completing my mission; too little would lead to the same result. Like Goldilocks, I chose the exact right size of soul for this human incarnation. Not too much; not too little, but just right. The Twelve, who understood this acutely, were careful not to overpower that small part of my soul that existed in my earth form. They entered slowly, carefully; they might *burn me out* I heard more than once.

"What would prevent you from completing your mission?" Douglas asked.

"Too much joy," I answered. "It's strength, but it can make you too soft to live effectively in this existence," I explained. "So we agreed that only a small part would incarnate, and my dad's mission was to focus the joy as a strength and not allow the joy to contribute to any weakness. I'm an introvert at heart," I said as an example of how my father prepared me for my mission.

As I spoke the words to Douglas, I saw scene after scene from my own life of my father encouraging me to speak; sometimes he offered his spare change in exchange for words. Sometimes, when I avoided a righteous conflict, he let me stew in my own shame. I struggled with the lesson. It was not something that came naturally to me. I was the quiet one of the family, the non-fighter, the peace maker. Anger did not hold me long enough to result in an argument; instead, I retreated at the first sign of a dispute. But my father understood there would be times when it was necessary for me to speak up, and he needed to teach me that anger and strength of conviction were not the same; in general, avoiding anger was a good goal for a joyful life, but avoiding justifiable conflict was a weakness that led to unhappiness. Strength required good trouble, and my father taught me this through pocket-change bribes. For the most part, it worked. As I accepted his money, I learned when it was appropriate to engage.

"My dad said it was money well spent; now I should give *him* money," I chuckled.

As I continued to narrate the story of my family for Douglas, other scenes were playing out for me. Sometimes simultaneously. They piled up, so I'd have to explain the concurrent scenes after I watched them. Things happened so quickly—and so out of time—that I could not keep up with the narration for Douglas. Time, I was learning, was an earth concept; it did not exist in the timelessness of the spirit world, so narratives started and finished and started again without any clear order. As I narrated my life story for Douglas, I had already moved on to another spectacle in the spirit world.

Standing fully in the shimmering light of Archangel Michael, I watched as each of the other archangels entered. There was a palpable silence, an awe; shared thoughts were suspended as each glorious light being made their way to a semi-circle behind a physically absent, but no less substantial podium. I sensed the podium rather than saw it, in other words. When the archangels had arranged themselves, they began to link with each other. Light burst with each connection. They radiated so bright that the center grew dark and a halo of light created an aura around them.

While I stood in the warm light of Michael and watched the spectacle of the other twelve archangels, he slowly, gently released me and made his way to the group. Michael, the thirteenth archangel, took his place, and the magnificence of the twelve already-connected archangels grew a thousand-fold as Michael took his place. A sonic boom radiated out from the angelic group. I could hear it, and I could see the soundwaves moving outwards from them. The effect, however, was a pleasant one, a gentle warmth blowing through the crowd of light beings, all of us bathed in a feeling of utter and complete and selfless love.

Michael is the plug to the matrix, the light beings explained, and although I did not consciously understand their explanation, I did understand at some deeper, forgotten level. It was like that. Somewhere I already knew what I couldn't explain. I simply didn't have the words or the ability in human form to make it concrete. This understanding didn't upset me, however. I was also aware that I would have all the understanding I needed in order to spread the message that would save humanity from itself.

"I had five brothers and sisters who were loud. And funny. And fighters," I continued my narrative for Douglas as I watched the archangel spectacle. "They put me with them specifically, so I could learn to stand my ground. Because what we are about to do is going to be hard," I announced.

"Do you know what is referenced when that is said?" Douglas asked.

"The message. The message is going to be hard," I answered.

"Do you have a sense of why it will be hard?"

"Because the earthly me will feel this is," I said and stopped to regroup. "I need to recognize that the message is hard, but the results can be joy. I can't get stuck in the message. That's where I've always been. Stuck in the message."

As I spoke to Douglas, I understood the problem The Twelve were trying to convey.

You are afraid of the message because you do not see what could be, they said.

I had already been shown the chaos the earth would face if we did not change our path. I had always known or, at least, had always sensed the potential for chaos and had avoided listening to guidance from the spirit world. I also feared being ostracized for delivering such a message. I still do. Speaking truth had led to lives of loneliness and, at least twice, death; I had already been shown this in past life regressions. Naturally, I didn't want to face being ostracized again in this lifetime.

It is your agreement, I heard whispered in response to my fears.

"The Twelve are here. Everybody's watching. Now it's my choice to come to them," I explained to Douglas.

"Is this a good time to get stage fright?" he asked, apparently reading my feelings.

Douglas's joke broke my rising fear. At least temporarily.

"I'm in Michael's light. He's right with me," I explained.

"Good."

"Momentous. It's a momentous moment," I said. "The light beings are here to watch. I don't know why."

"I would suspect that this is one of your very significant agreements that you have to accomplish in this life," Douglas tried to explain.

"Yes," I responded in a little girl's faraway voice. "It's my first big one," I clarified. "They're funny," I said in reference to The Twelve; "they say they're the real Illuminati."

As the group of twelve entered, my gaze was guided to the physical realm, to earth. I sat suspended above the earth, anchored to something physical. I was still in the spirit world and Douglas's office, but now I was also suspended just above the earth in what we casually, theatrically call outer space. I saw ships. One was like an aircraft carrier; another was hidden in a heat shield. Once I was directed to look in its direction, I could see the radiation from the shield. If I squinted my eyes, I saw the ship too. Some ships were camouflaged by stars. Some ships were built for larger sentient beings; others were tiny for the smallest of beings. Interestingly, I understood the science of it all although I hadn't spent any time in formal study. On the spirit side, I absorbed and understood the physics of it all; it was as obvious as two plus two. While I reveled in my new understanding,

I also had a sense of fear as I looked towards the earth. It was not the type of fear that would paralyze me in life. Rather, I had a vague notion the earth was facing a turning point. The ships were on stand-by, but I did not understand why. Not until later. Not until the danger had all but passed.

They are the star people. Stellars, I heard.

"Are they in spirit?" I asked.

They are physical. Just different, I heard in response.

I had the sense of being a child; the others in the arena smiled sweetly in that way that said *how quaint.* When I used vocal cords to speak, they shook their heads and smiled some more. While I understood the concept that I could speak through my thoughts, I didn't quite know how. I found it hard to initiate a conversation, for example, so I reverted to what I knew on earth: vocal chords. And to the Stellars, it must have been like hearing an opera through an old scratchy-sounding gramophone.

You will learn, The Twelve assured me.

"All the archangels have just joined," I announced to Douglas long after I had seen it happen. The spectacle repeated itself so that I could describe it accurately. It was as if I was seeing a rerun. "Ah, they're magnificent! They...."

"Kind of bright?"

"But they link together," I explained. "There's a harmonic. There's a pulsing energy. A harmonic. A majesty of the archangels. And Michael's about to join."

In the moment that I included Douglas in what I was re-seeing, Michael filled me with his radiance. It was as if he had placed his hand on my shoulder to calm me, to reassure me.

"If you can imagine a comforting sonic boom," I told Douglas.

"Really big, but very comforting, huh?" he asked.

"Majesty is all I can think. And when they link together, they become a whole. They create the bosom of the power. I don't know what that means. They create the bosom of the power," I repeated.

"Hmm."

"And it's my choice. They won't suck my soul into The Twelve. I need to make the choice as a physical being."

When The Twelve arrived fully, I was read a list of rules or potential outcomes of agreeing to accept the message of human salvation. I would give voice to that message. While the spirit beings around me did not have discernible mouths or respiratory systems, I felt as if the collective was holding its breath, waiting for me to decide.

If you accept, the group of twelve read to me, *you will lose physical years.*

I felt tears burn my physical, human cheeks as the rules were read.

If you hold the message in your heart, there will be breast cancer. If you hold it in your stomach with worry, there will be stomach cancer.

With each proclamation, I felt more fear; in fact, I became paralyzed with it. The group of twelve spoke the rules in such blasé fashion. *Meh. What's a few years?* their tone conveyed. *Eh. It's all temporary anyway.* As their list of rules were read, I found my way to their tone. *Meh,* I thought, *breast cancer. Of course, it will manifest if I hold pain in my heart, so I won't. Meh.*

The Twelve spoke as one, but there were millions of layers of other voices that resonated from within their oneness. Souls. Millions of souls united in one message. When The Twelve spoke, the cacophony of sound pacified my single beating soul. Eventually the voice of my soul blended with theirs, and as part of the group, the message guided me to *meh*; when their guidance ended, however, I reevaluated what was being asked of me, and my fear returned. So, too, did my individuality as a soul voice, and I thought of myself as human again, not part of a spirit whole. *Give up some of my physical years,* I thought, and the thought led to tears.

"Let me know if you need my assistance," Douglas offered.

"I'm afraid," I announced to Douglas and then told him about the rules. Not all of them, of course, but the ones that frightened me the most.

"So, take a moment," he reassured me. "What is the fear of?"

"They told me the cost."

"And what is that?"

"Losing some years from my physical life," I said and, then, tried to explain. "It's like looking into the sun. Of course, there's a cost. You lose something. And I'll see the chaos."

"You mean as in seeing it in the future?"

"Yes."

"Yeah. So what can allay your fear?"

"I'll do it. I just need to feel it; I'm human," I explained. "I just need to feel the fear and then, move. They know I'm going to do it."

"Yeah. I do understand that," Douglas responded. "But my fonder hope for you is that you can move forward in the most comfortable way. So, as you get the bigger picture—and you know that you will—you'll know it's what you agreed to and what your soul wants to do," he explained. "Can you let Michael take the fear? It doesn't serve; it just distracts you," Douglas instructed me.

"I have to stay grounded because when I start to hear my voice speaking the words of the message of wisdom, I'll question everything."

What I meant to convey to Douglas is that I would question my own sanity, and I do. But I know when I'm in that other place—home—there is a confident *me* that loses itself in the singular dynamic of The Twelve. There is also a physical me that cowers like a child in a corner. *Oh my God*, I hear my earth psyche, *what must Douglas think of me?* In one part of my mind—my physical mind, I worry that Douglas will diagnose me or, more importantly, that he should.

"Well, that's your mind," Douglas tried to calm me. "So, I'm just going to throw this out to you as something that has worked well for me. When I'm really having to stay in a space and not have my mind do its mind thing, I have my mind go sit in Archangel Michael's lap."

"He's connected. He's linked," I said rejecting his advice.

I feared that Michael would be too busy to hold my mind. Before I could go into a full-blown panic, however, I understood I was interpreting Douglas's advice using earth rules. In the spiritual realm, Michael could do two things at once; in fact, he could do an infinite number of things at once, and I relinquished the burden of my mind to him.

"There are thirteen [archangels]," I told Douglas.

"Is Michael the thirteenth?"

"Yeah. And he's—it's not the right way to say this—but he's the power. He's the plug in the grid."

"So is your mind willing to sit in Michael's lap?"

"Yes."

As Douglas spoke, I instinctively looked to the archangel who stood united as one with the other twelve. Though a huge, illumined column of light, I sensed a nod from him. He already had it.

"I just think your mind can relax because we're totally protected, and your mind can kick back and enjoy the joy of being in Michael's lap."

As Douglas spoke, I remembered the images of the Stellars I had been shown earlier. As I thought about them, I instantaneously returned to watching them.

"I have to tell you something interesting they showed me. This is for you, too. The universe knows. The star people—the Stellars—are waiting. Somewhere right above. Right above the earth plane."

"Mmm," Douglas responded as if he were not surprised. To tell the truth; I was surprised by his lack of surprise.

"They're just waiting. They felt the power of the archangels connect. They know."

I was embarrassed by what I was describing, especially to a mental health professional. *Who would believe this stuff?* I thought to myself. I understood that the Stellars, who were simply physical entities but who were more advanced than humans, were waiting to see the results of the spirit world's celebration. Because they were more attuned to the spiritual realm, they understood that earth stood at a precipice.

Before humans could negatively impact the universe, I was told by one of the Stellar leaders, *they would destroy the earth.*

In one possible future scenario, I saw the shot; I saw the earth instantly and irrevocably vaporized. The Stellars were waiting for some evidence that they should stand down. They were waiting for a sign from the archangels.

"Your friend is in the waiting position. He's letting you know," I informed Douglas.

"Golodor?" Douglas asked.

"Yeah," I said uncomfortable with the whole Stellar conversation.

"Yeah," Douglas tried to assure me.

"He's letting you know."

"I appreciate that," Douglas sighed.

"Move her forward, he says."

"What was that?"

"Move her forward, he says."

"OK. So, are you ready to move forward?"

You need to make the choice to join us, The Twelve told me. *You must take the steps to join. It is a physical choice.*

I stood knowing full well that I would make the decision to join The Twelve, but I was also paralyzed with fear at the thought of it. In an effort to help me, they showed me memories of my human life where they had trained me for this exact moment. I saw a series of events that had always had some significance for me even if I couldn't explain why. One happened when I was a little girl.

When I was eleven years old, I stood on the high-dive at Knoebel's Grove Amusement Park in my green and blue Scottish-kilt-patterned two-piece. Long dark hair and blunt-cut bangs blew in the slight breeze above the crowded pool. My friends stood bunched up on the ladder to the high dive. They were waiting—not so patiently—for me to jump.

"C'mon. Go!" one kid yelled.

My legs shook with fear as I turned to see my classmates waving me on, laughing, their bodies stacked on the ladder, blocking my way back to safety. *Why aren't they scared?* I thought. I was amazed at their tenacity, especially in

21

comparison to my own fear. The lifeguard's whistle blew to my left. I turned my body slowly on the plank and moved my eyes to the sound of the whistle. White-nosed and red-trunked, the blonde-headed lifeguard waved me on. He sat slouched in his high wooden chair, his head swiveling from left to right and from right to left, watching all the bodies in the pool.

"Jackie, go!" I heard from behind me, but I was too scared to turn.

I inched my way to the front of the board. I knew I would jump. I knew I would. I just didn't want to. There was nowhere to go but off the diving board. The bodies in the pool did not seem to notice me standing over them, watching them. I scanned the patchwork of blankets for my mother; when I found her, she was a polka-dotted clad speck in the crowd. She did not notice me either.

"Is she scared or what?" one of the boys on the diving board stairs yelled.

The whistle blew again, and I turned in its direction. My feet pointed left off the board. The moment was near, I knew, and I did not have the ability to turn my feet to face the front of the diving board. There was nothing left to do but jump, yet I held my place just a bit longer, stuck in a fear-induced inertia.

"C'mon Jackie," one of my friends whined. "Just do it."

Years later, when I was a principal of an elementary school, the fire department showed up for fire safety day with a hook and ladder truck.

"Wanna climb up the ladder?" the chief asked. "You know . . . the kids would love it."

No, I thought honestly, as I scanned the faces of the Kindergartners and First Graders sitting cross-legged on the front lawn of the school. The flagpole stood in the middle, and I looked up to see the flag waving furiously; the end of the hook and ladder swayed in the air, matching the movement of the flag. The sight did not instill confidence in me, and I was prepared to tell the chief that I would not comply with his request. Until it was too late to tell him.

"Do you want your principal to climb the ladder?" the chief asked through his bullhorn.

"Yeaaaah," the kids responded, their eyes popping, their heads swiveling to talk to their neighbors.

I knew I would do it. I knew I would. But, for the moment, I was paralyzed with fear. Before I began my ascent up the twenty-five-foot ladder, swaying in the early November wind, I thought of the moment when I stood on the diving board at Knoebel's Grove, looking over the left edge, hearing the voices of other pre-teens behind me, pushing me, angling for their turns on the high dive.

As I stood on the board with my friends yelling and the lifeguard whistling and the bodies in the pool ignoring my private drama, I understood that the jump was inevitable. I was meant to jump. Just like years later when I was the principal of an elementary school on fire safety day, I was meant to climb. It was inevitable. Both events were meant to teach me. I was meant to commit. So, I did.

I stood paralyzed with fear in front of the The Twelve. The collective breath of light beings waited, federation ships hung suspended above the earth, the archangels continued to radiate a sonic boom, the group of twelve nodded their belief in me. I knew it was inevitable; I would make the physical choice to join them despite the potential physical danger to me. I knew I would commit just like I knew I would jump from the high dive at Knoebel's Grove and climb the ladder on fire safety day at the elementary school. So, I did.

Although there were no steps, I climbed my way to the group of twelve. A spirit hand—I don't know whose—held my hand as I made my way. It was a physical journey. It was meant to be a physical journey. I had to *feel* what I was about to do. I had to *feel* it. When I reached the top, The Twelve repeated the rules and the potential physical issues. What should have taken days to read, took a fraction of a second. I heard them read it, but in a time radically compacted.

The no-air in the forum of millions of spirit beings calmed. A thumping in my ears increased as my heart pounded out its disinclination to commit.

I felt the weight of the universe in my decision, so I shook my head *yes*. And my hand was moved to the collective hand of The Twelve. The earth time that had heretofore constrained me stopped. I was one with The Twelve, and worlds opened up before me.

"I'm home," I whimpered. "I'm home. And she's accepted. She's accepted," I said, referring to my physical body. "It will burn her up a little early, but she's accepted."

All that I had been, all that I am, and all that I ever will be played out in front of me. The light beings gathered breath, a celebration rose, my dad nodded in something akin to pride, the energy from the archangels shifted and changed, the fleet above the earth were moved to stand down. Collective relief. Joy. Earth, though shaken up with the energy of the day, would stand. At least for a while more.

A weighted blanket of calm spread over me. The physical disappeared as I was consumed into The Twelve. I felt my place among them, and although my ego continued to wage war—driven by fear, as it was—I was able to keep sending it back to the archangel's lap as Douglas had suggested.

Do not interpret our words, I heard myself in chorus with the others tell the ego. It was not a warning. There was no implicit threat. Only instruction. *You will learn. Trust will build*, I heard. It was inevitable. It was meant to be. Jump off the board. Climb up the ladder. Commit to your destiny. Trust in what will be.

"And so, it is," I announced to Douglas after I accepted the challenge of my life's mission.

A Message from The Twelve:
The Connectedness of all Things

"Now you know the questions to ask," said a calmer, more mature voice.

The sentence was directed at Douglas who had not yet noticed the shift. It was my voice—sort of—coming from my mouth, but it was no longer me speaking. It was a strange, disorienting moment. In my mind's eye, I saw myself sitting in the corner of a room watching as my body was taken over. While it wasn't *physical* at all, a new, very powerful awareness settled in and pushed my human psyche to the side. I understood the voice speaking through me as not one voice, but a chorus of voices, a multitude of conscious entities merged into one voice that spoke through me. The Twelve were part of the merged entities; in fact, they distilled the other spirit voices into one and took responsibility for guiding the interactions. I had the distinct sense The Twelve were crowdsourcing, and I've since learned that my impression was not far from the truth. *As above, so below,* as it goes.

"You know the questions," the voice repeated for Douglas's benefit.

"I do, huh?" Douglas asked.

"Listen to your guidance," she said. The voice projected a female aspect. At least to me.

Silence ensued. Not just a pause, but a long, torturous hush.

Ask a question, Douglas, I wanted to scream out, but could not.

Patience, The Twelve whispered. *He is finding his destiny.*

25

While the merged spirits maintained an expectant serenity; I could not. I felt panicked as time ticked away. While time on the other side is non-existent, I experienced the wait through the restrictions of the time-centered notions I have accepted in this human incarnation. So, as the merged spirits waited for Douglas to respond to the prompt, I experienced the spirit plane's timelessness as the equivalent of days, weeks, maybe even months of earth time while the time in Douglas's office registered only a few minutes. The cost of merging with The Twelve—the loss of a few human years, as I originally understood it—had been misinterpreted by me. I would spend those years. All of them. Just some of them on the spirit side. With each spirit interaction, timelessness took its toll on my human body as it stretched into compacted, sensory-rich segments. In other words, I lived larger chunks of time on the spirit side than what the clock measured in Douglas's office. Still, I lived them. There was no loss in the decision to merge.

As with anything I experienced in the spirit world, I was constrained by the words and understandings of my current human experiences; in other words, I could not fully comprehend and depict concepts as accurately as I would like. Like explaining timelessness, for example. Humans are not advanced enough to contemplate experiences outside their current contrived views of the cosmos, and they certainly do not have the language to represent what they cannot see and accept. As if wearing blinders, we are immune to the evidence all around us. At least for the time being.

"Feel the vibration," the voice finally said to Douglas, breaking the long silence. "Feel the change in vibration. She's not alone today," the voice said referring to me. "There are others."

With her statement, Douglas knew he was talking to another entity and would begin to interact with her, not me. I, too, began to interact with the voice of the merged spirits. Quietly. Internally. There were big questions—the-secret-of-the-universe type kind—and there were small-ish questions. I asked about specific moments in my life: the loss of my first child to a late miscarriage, the end of a marriage, my exile to the Middle East; such questions were of little consequence to the workings of the greater universe, but they were important to me and so they were honored. *What were these experiences meant to teach me?* I asked. *Why did they happen?* With patience and understanding, the voice of the merged spirits answered the questions I could comprehend. For those I could not, she told me, *as you become more and more aware, you will understand more.*

And although I could not explain it from the perspective of my earth incarnation, somewhere I understood what she meant. Not on the surface, of course, but somewhere deep inside me a tiny spring of almost-understanding sprung up. I knew—though I didn't know how I knew—my answers would come, not as new knowledge, but as a sort of *remembering*, and I was satisfied that I could wait. As I asked and answered my questions, the voice simultaneously responded to a question Douglas had not asked. At least, not out loud.

"Yes. We are higher than counsel if you need to know in earth terms," the voice responded. "We are higher than counsel."

"Counsel?" Douglas asked. "I don't know the reference to *counsel.*"

"Higher than counsel. Higher than archangels. Even when they are joined," the voice explained.

"My goodness," Douglas said.

"Wisdom," the voice named itself.

"That's kind of humbling."

"No. No," she said. It just is," the voice corrected. "We create the vibrations. The harmonics."

"Of the very universe?" Douglas asked.

"Yes."

"Yes," Douglas repeated.

"Yes," the voice said again. "And beyond."

At this point in the conversation, fear had attempted to reassert its will, my ego. After all, the voice was using my body. *I have a right to participate,* I told The Twelve.

"If she interprets, it will *not* come out right," they said to Douglas, but it was meant as a mild rebuke to me as well.

"Right," Douglas answered.

"So, you have to correct her."

"To not interpret?" he asked.

"To not interpret. As we give the message, do not interpret. Interpretation will come later," she promised. "We will help."

"I get that. I was wondering about that," Douglas said. "So, when it starts to flow, just stand aside and let it flow?"

"Yes. She'll have trouble with that," the voice said, referring to me. "In the beginning."

"Yes."

"She's fighting already," the voice affirmed.

Feeling rebuked by the back and forth, I finally relented, relinquished my ego to the archangels, and listened. Simply listened. Yet as questions emerged in my thoughts—even in the midst of the conversation with Douglas, they were answered.

After a long pause, the voice continued, "Earth is part of the matrix of sound and color. Of light. When the matrix is disturbed at one level, it is disturbed at all levels. Like a hologram," she explained. Humanity is a disturbance; not of its own accord," the voice of merged spirits warned. "And it will destroy the matrix if it's not destroyed first. But there's time," she conceded. "Like when there are cancer cells that affect the being, and the cancer cells are eliminated so that the being can be healthy. If the cells are not destroyed, the being dies," the voice explained with a metaphor. "And that is the progression of earth right now," she said. "You have the tools. Just not the recognition of the tools. We can offer vibration, and we can offer the message, but it is for you to find the tools and use them. That's your free will."

He thinks you're one spirit, I said. *"Tell him how many are in the one voice,"* I pleaded.

After a long pause in which we discussed the importance of Douglas knowing how many spirit voices were involved in the message, she began to speak again, "she wants us to tell you about the millions of voices in one. It's possible that you can hear it too. That is why we are *we*," she said, marking the collective in the single voice. "You may ask," the voice advised Douglas.

"When you said it was up to you to use the tools, who was the *you*?"

"Humanity."

"OK," Douglas responded.

"And though you're not part of this world normally," the voice said, "you are now. In this incarnation."

"By hook or by crook, yes," Douglas laughed.

What? I thought, stunned by the turn in the conversation. In the moment of this back and forth between Douglas and the merged spirit voice, I stopped asking my own questions to listen more intently. That he was not "part of this world normally" was accepted by Douglas as a matter of fact, and it seemed strange to me. In fact, it scared me a little. *What did he know?*

What did he mean by that? I asked the voice that spoke through me.

The answer will come, she replied. *On his terms.*

And simultaneously, she responded to Douglas, "by your *own* decision," the voice said. It was both a reminder to him of his past agreements and a joke.

"So I get reminded," Douglas laughed.

"They remind you often, I hear," the voice ribbed him.

"Incessantly."

"Yes. Golodor is from the council of elders," the voice affirmed a question that Douglas had not yet asked.

"He's from *my* council of elders?"

"Yes."

"He has a hard job," she teased.

"What makes it so hard?"

"The denseness of this area," she replied meaning the earth realm.

"Mm-hmm."

"We ask much. We ask much of the light that's trapped in dense bodies" the voice explained to Douglas.

"Can you expand on that?" Douglas asked.

"Can I expand on . . .? On what we ask?"

"When you talked about *you ask much of light trapped in dense bodies*," Douglas clarified.

"Yes. You and others are here as light warriors from all over the universe and beyond. You know each other. You may have passed a fellow light bearer . . . a fellow light warrior . . . and recognized him or her without knowing the body that he or she inhabits," she said. "You are aware of each other. You've come to bring a vibration, but only some part of your light can inhabit the physical bodies, and so often, hard times and difficult choices have faced you as we reach out to remind you of your mission," she said. "Maybe a few have thought that the universe is unfair, but you signed up for that as well. For the warnings. For the reminders of your mission. Your mission is very simply to save humanity," she said matter-of-factly. "They are on the brink," she warned. "This is a beautiful existence. A wonderful experiment. But the souls in the physical bodies were corrupted; it has created trouble. The souls will survive. But we're not sure that the race will. You may ask why there is such an effort to save one race, and that would be a good question."

"Mm," Douglas agreed.

"We know that this life is temporary, but we know that the soul can be damaged from pain, from trauma," the voice explained. "It affects their movement through the light. Their progression. And so, it is a worthy goal to save humanity, to save the souls from the damage. With what is coming, it could be millennia before the souls are strong enough to go out again. But it's also a radiating effect, and that's why the Stellars are worried about this as well," she said re-introducing the group into her explanation. "It will affect the hologram—the matrix—and other souls will be bruised as well.

But if the light warriors . . . if they succeed . . . you will have raised the souls to a new level, and that new level sends a vibration through the rest of the universe and beyond. So, it is worthy," she finished "And now she feels joy," the voice said referring to me. "Now she understands."

As Douglas waited, over a minute of silence ensued as the voice let the weight of her words sink in. She and the other spirits—including The Twelve—had waited millennia to deliver the message; they would take their time now to make sure it was understood. But they would not wait for long. The cost of the connection to The Twelve began to take its toll on me. I felt hot. My throat burned. I began to cough, and they reconnected with Douglas.

"Do you fear us?" the merged spirits asked Douglas.

Yes! I screamed out in my head. The ego had begun its work of reminding me about other incarnations. Telling my truth had gotten me ousted from groups and, in rare instances, killed in two different incarnations by one who had tried to quiet me.

The Twelve smiled and nodded to the archangel Michael. He enfolded me in his light, and the ego slowly shut down. With it, my fear flamed out.

"Probably," Douglas responded. "I don't even know if I understand what that's about, but it's a fair question."

"You will find signs in your life that will help you accept, but it's possible you'll never believe. And that's okay."

"If I don't believe, what is it I won't believe?" he asked.

"You believe in the higher realm. And you believe in other worlds, but it will still gnaw at you because you're human," the voice explained. "And that's something you should not worry about. That should not be a reason to stop moving forward."

"Right." Douglas said.

"Determine each step. Each step. One step at a time," the voice instructed. "Don't worry about ten steps ahead. You'll decide at each step."

"I presume that you are an emanation of Source?"

"Of course."

"Okay."

"As are you."

"Fair enough," Douglas conceded.

"Do you need us to explain it?"

"Um, sure. That would be helpful," Douglas agreed.

"The power is the matrix . . . both the creator of and, itself, the matrix. On the matrix, is every star system, every planet, every universe, every physical entity, every soul. It all emanates from one. It's the one," her explanation began. "We are holograms of the Source. And we progress towards the reality of goodness and vibration and understanding. If you think of the aura of the sun as the physical part of the matrix, you can understand that it's not the sun, and it is the sun at the same time," she explained through metaphor. "It is the aura of the sun, connected and not connected at the same time. Force and not force at the same time. And that is us. And that is you. And that is Source," the voice explained.

My mind moved back into control, and my physicality reasserted itself. I felt hot, overwhelmed. My throat was tight, and my cough became more insistent.

"Her thoughts are intruding," the voice disclosed.

"I'm sorry?" Douglas asked for clarification.

"Her thoughts are intruding."

"Can we get your mind to go back into Michael's lap?" he suggested.

"She does not know the message yet. She knows the result of the path the earth is currently on. We will bring the message forward little by little. It will overwhelm her," she explained. After a long pause, the voice continued, "she has a soul name that sounds in earth language like *Akia*, and it comforts her. But it's not exactly that sound. But she can hear the rest of it."

"So Akia?" Douglas asked.

"Akia. Not Ikea."

"So, it's with an *ah*?"

"*She* asked about Ikea," the voice joked referring to my last question.

Moments later the voice recognized the physical toll of my connection with The Twelve. *It's time*, she said.

No, I protested; *I'm fine*. Even as I said it, I knew the decision had already been made. By The Twelve. And by me.

"Enough," the voice said to Douglas. "Enough."

"Enough for today?" he clarified.

"Yes."

"Thank you for coming forward," Douglas said.

"We are pleased."

"I would like to believe it will be more fun," Douglas added.

"For sure," the fading response came.

The Twelve moved its focus from me to the archangels. The physical me was released from the soul connection, and the steps to the physical world re-appeared. I wanted to stay; I begged to stay.

You cannot, the voice said clearly; *you have a mission*.

There would be no off-ramp for me. This I understood form her words. I had committed, and I would finish the mission I had accepted almost a millennium ago. On the verge of a child-like temper-tantrum, she threw her light around me in embrace. *You have a mission*, she whispered over and over again as the steps to the physical world came closer.

"You can call us the Illuminati until we reveal our names," the merged spirits said to Douglas. And when he didn't respond, they added, "that's humor."

Douglas laughed, "Yes, it is."

"The archangel is un-twinned, and he will bring her back."

The physical me watched the magnificence of Archangel Michael's light re-establishing its individuality. The collective light of the other archangels dimmed noticeably; the energy they resonated when they were linked slowly dissipated into a chorus of different vibrations. The archangel's light poured over and through me, and I closed my eyes and lifted my face to drink it in. I was being prepared—cleansed almost—to reenter the physical world.

You have done well, I heard from The Twelve. *Go now.*

And I did. I moved up the floating steps and through the door to the physical world, but a large part of me remained behind, and I knew it was as it should be.

ACT II

Gift from God

30 May 2019

Just above our terror, the stars painted this story in perfect silver calligraphy. And our souls, too often abused by ignorance, covered our eyes with mercy.
Aberjhani

To Believe or Not To Believe;
That is the Question

Touch has a memory.

~John Keats

In the seven days between sessions, I believed absolutely in all I had seen and heard and experienced under hypnosis. I knew, without a doubt, I had been in the spirit realm, and I understood unquestionably what had transpired and what had been communicated to me. For the first couple of days after the first session, I dreamt of the soft lilac and fire orange of the day-into-night sky; in my waking hours, I walked through fields of sage and lavender, hands outstretched to purposely disturb the stalks, hoping to conjure up the perfume of the other world, and I tried to recall the pleasant, totally present feeling of communicating without words.

By day three, when thoughts of Stellars and their floating, heat-shielded ships invaded the idyllic of the spirit scenes, however, I reevaluated my experiences as cringe-worthy, ridiculous, maybe even a little crazy. It did not take long, then, for me to stop believing absolutely.

"Oh my God," I told my son, "I've been writing about ancient astronauts."

While I expected more concern or at the least, a little angst, he was completely unfazed by the topic. His shock was reserved for another point altogether. He was concerned that I even questioned whether humans shared the universe with other sentient beings.

"You don't think we're the only ones, do you?" he asked in a way that suggested what my answer should be. "I'd be pretty disappointed if we didn't find proof of other civilizations sometime in my life," he added. "Wouldn't you?"

"I don't think we're the only ones in the universe, Collin," I said. "I just don't want to be the one to tell everyone."

What I feared as I wrote the first session was that my overly left-brained existence would be rocked by such an admission. Stellars? Really? In light of my conversation with Collin, however, I reconsidered it. *Why not?* I asked. The conversation with my son had triggered another round of believing. And when I had finally settled firmly and absolutely on believing again, the day of the next hypnotic session rolled around, and I swung back to not believing. The whole episode reminded me of a healer I had met a few years earlier in Dubai.

I had read about her in an unusual place, *The Gulf News*. It was unusual because I had hardly ever read *The Gulf News* and, to be honest, because her line of work was something not openly discussed in the UAE papers. Her name was Seda. She was Turkish from Zimbabwe, but lived in Dubai in a place where you can almost, but not quite, see the deep blue of the gulf. The writer of the *Gulf* article went to see Seda as a skeptic, but left gushing about her healing abilities. He could not exactly say what Seda had done, but he felt strangely changed, and that was enough for me. I had just finished listening to a book about past life regressions on my daily one-to-three-hour drive to and from Dubai, and I was hooked on the concept of energy healing.

While many people may not understand the attraction to such practices, I have long been open to the alternative. I was sure healing would be good for me; there were too many inexplicable behavioral patterns and fears that could not be banished—or even diminished—with logic. So I looked for answers. When all conventional avenues seemed to have dead-ended, an energy healer seemed somehow sensible.

"So what type of energy work would you like?" Seda asked.

"I don't know."

I assumed she saw an exhausted woman at the end of a workday in brick-red harem pants, a white t-shirt, and black sweater. Before I could apologize for not being more prepared, she spoke.

"You're beautiful."

For weeks, I had been unusually upset with the ageing process. Looking into the mirror, I saw a face I no longer knew, a face that at fifty seemed to have lost its elasticity, its youth, its long-held confines of cheeks and chin, eyes and forehead. Everything now seemed to be merging along a growing network of etchings and wrinkles. Her compliment gave me a much-needed lift.

"Your eyes. They're beautiful."

"Oh, thank you," I said, suddenly understanding. My eyes. People often noticed the light, light, gray-blue of them. Like my dad's. And when they comment on them, they bring my father back into focus, a lovely gift, him having passed away a few years ago now. I understood the compliment as a sign that seeing Seda was a good idea.

"What type of healing do you do?" I asked as if I would understand.

As she rattled off many of the same specialties as the author of my recent book, Seda made me feel increasingly comfortable. So in the end, I let her choose the type of healing for me. Shamanic healing, it was. Her specialty. I laid flat on her divan, covered in a southwestern-style blanket, a blindfold over my eyes. In the background, indigenous music from around the world played.

"Do you give me permission to perform whatever healing is best for your highest self?"

"Yes," I stammered.

Although I could not see, I felt and heard the swoosh of feathers from a ceremonial fan above me. Seda chanted. Incense burned. A Tibetan singing bowl sang out its tone-rich song. Across the street, a mosque added its melody as the *Call to Prayer* issued forth. A candle warmed the pads of my bared feet, and the sacred oil of Peru anointed my forehead, nose, chin. Despite all the commotion, however, I fell asleep and only awoke when, shortly before the end of the session, I was startled by my own loud snore.

"So?" Seda asked.

"I dreamt," I responded honestly, a little embarrassed I had fallen asleep. And snored.

"What did you dream?"

"There was a small group of light beings—maybe five or six. I couldn't make out features, but they had arms and legs and heads like us."

"Go on," she urged.

"I felt them put their hands underneath me. They were all around this divan," I pointed below me, "and then they raised me up in the air."

"And?" Seda urged.

"And I felt so light, so loved. All pain disappeared. They fixed me."

"Yes, they healed you. I saw them, too," she said and went on to explain the movements of the beings whom I had seen in my dream.

"But it was a dream," I protested.

"Was it?" she asked.

Seda explained that the light beings were my soul family; we had all originated in another star system: "the Pleiades," she said as if it were something normal to say. *Makes sense,* I thought considering all the times I had felt out-of-step on earth. Until I considered the logic of the episode and convinced myself that it didn't. Even though I experienced it—even then—I wavered. This is what it is to be human.

The Second Hypnotic Session: Going Home to The Pleiades

When Douglas began the count to still my mind and begin the hypnotic process, I was full of doubt, anxiety even. Maybe my ego would resist; maybe I would resist. *I do not believe in hypnosis,* I told myself over and over again, and I wondered, even as Douglas coached me to relax, if he would be able to fool me once again into hypnosis. I was convinced that my last foray had been a fluke and that it would forever remain my last foray into hypnosis.

As I closed my eyes and Douglas started to count, my predictions seemed accurate. Unlike the first time, no one joined me on the first step to my sacred space. Not Archangel Michael and not my spirit guide, Willie. I was all alone in a panorama of endless black; the floating, backlit, unattached staircase was all I could see; there was nothing and no one else. My mind shouted: *It's not going to work. It's not going to work. This isn't real.* But when Douglas reached two, I calmed, found my center, and was on my way to the sacred space.

"Three. Deeper. Deeper. Easier and deeper," Douglas continued until I reached the door to the spirit world. "Ten. Deep. Deeper. Deepest. You're at the door to your sacred space. Go ahead and open it. Step through," he said. "Go ahead and close the door behind you and move into your sacred space." After a long silence, he added, "And whenever you're ready, just let me know what's going on."

"I'll spend some time on the physical," I told him after my own silence.

On the drive to Douglas's office on the morning of the second session, I had spoken out loud my intention to note the physical markers of the space I would inhabit during the hypnotic trance. In the first regression, I had perceived sounds and colors, but I had not paid enough attention to the setting to adequately describe it in writing. Some of this was due to the fact that many of the sounds and colors have no cognates here on earth. There are significantly more colors and significantly more vibrant hues in the spirit world; in addition to the colors, there is a humming harmonics-type particular signature to every being, every landform, even the atmosphere. If I were going to attempt to translate what I saw within the constraints of my physical language, I would need to pay better attention. So, I asked the spirit world to guide me.

As I walked through the door to my sacred space, I recognized home. My *star* home. Although this sounds really odd, my soul is tied to another star system, as is Douglas's. We are neighbors, he and I. I am a Stellar at the soul level, but I agreed to be incarnated on earth. In a past life, I had accepted a mission that might help save humanity. *No small task there; no pressure at all.* By incarnating as a human, the task—or the mission—became an *insider's* job, and my knowledge of humanity could be used to improve the chances of success. It was not the first time in earth's history that spirit incarnated to help save the world. And, in fact, I was around for that incarnation, too. As an apprentice. Two thousand years ago. In the spirit world, two thousand years is not a lot of time; think eons and millennia and eternity for some comparison. Thus, my apprenticeship is not as far apart from my present incarnation as it might seem when considering the separation between them in earth years.

"There are two moons," I told Douglas. "From where I'm standing, they're here like this," I said, moving my hands to the left, one above the other in a slight diagonal.

One moon—the top one—was bigger and brighter; the bottom moon had a yellow tint. They appeared attached to one another because of the way the glow around them seemed to touch. The inky bluish-black sky in which they hung had dark lines of clouds, not the white clouds of earth. Instead, they were more gray, not as fluffy, and the light from the moons made them almost silver-like in their perch.

"They feel close like when we have a harvest moon here," I said, my voice distant, quieter than usual. "And we can move between them. Like visiting."

When hypnotized, my voice sounded faraway, the narration slower. Much slower. Silence filled the space between words and phrases; in fact, silence was the most notable part of the hypnosis. Unusually uncomfortable with silence, it took me some time to disengage my ego enough *not* to fill the space with my own words. I needed to learn to respect the no-time-ness of the other side by allowing silence.

"I have a sense that it's day, but it's not like it is here. It's lilac," I said. "The sky is like a greyish first and, then, it gradually moves into lilac. And then in the sky, I can see the stars. It's the same," I said and then stopped. "Well not the same look," I tried again, "but the same characteristics as the sky we look at."

The sun, I intuited, was further away from my home planet than our sun is from the earth. The colors, then, are not the earthy warm colors of yellows and oranges and browns; rather, the colors of my home planet reflect cooler winter colors. There are softer purples and blues, greys and muted greens although the sky, from time to time, has a bright orange horizon.

As I described the setting to Douglas, I sensed the presence of Michael. He was near. He was on guard, but for some reason, he allowed me stand alone as I cataloged the features and sounds, tastes and smells of an almost-known, almost-home place. The archangel does not leave me even in a non-hypnotic state. It's been this way lately. Even as I sleep, I feel Michael's presence, nearly physical, but not quite. I am rarely alone these days.

After a long silence in which I gathered the words to describe what I was seeing, I continued, "The air is thicker. But not humid. I don't mean humid. It's more condensed. More packed."

In the middle of the description, I whispered "Oh!" The exclamation was not at all related to what I was describing to Douglas. Instead, it marked the simultaneous conversations I was having with spirit beings. Not being fully reacquainted with the telepathy-ish communication of the spirit world, sometimes my other conversations momentarily broke into a physical narrative.

"We're . . . we're shaped differently," I began again. "Same basic shape, but more angular, taller. The backbone is much more defined. Like you can feel it," I explained as I made the outline of the backbone with my physical hand. "Tapered," I said finishing my description of what *we* look like.

I had the sense I was looking at someone I might have known from another existence. Maybe me. In fact, I was almost sure it was me. And like a science experiment, I examined the me in front of me. She did the same. There was nothing strange about the way we looked at each other—up and down, back and forth, like a trainer checking a horse's teeth; in fact, recognizing each other was actually comforting.

"There's a sound in the air. It's not this, but it's like at night . . . on a summer night . . . when the crickets are chirping. It's pleasant." When the me of the other world retreated, I realized there were no other entities on the planet except for me and the archangel. "I'm all alone," I said, a touch a panic in my voice. My ego had come calling.

As fear began to tighten my throat and my heart responded with increased beating, the archangel drew his light around me, and I responded immediately in palpable relief. With his light, understanding settled onto me, and I knew what lay before me. When he knew I understood, Michael stepped back to allow me to explore.

Thank you, I whispered.

"I'm all alone because I'm seeing an image," I explained to Douglas. "It's not the real place. They make it alive though," I added. "There are flowers,"

I said, sweeping my arm to the right. "Like a carpet of flowers. There are stems, but they are kind of grayish and lilac again just like the sky. They're pretty; just different."

As I spoke, Douglas listened. He did not interrupt; rather, he sat through long silences allowing me to spin out the description of another star system, another place, home. And as I spoke, I looked along the landscape for roads or buildings. There were long stretches of the natural world, as it appeared in this system, but no evidence of inhabitation.

Where do they live? I asked.

We live in houses, I heard in reply. Before the reply had finished, the structures materialized in front of me.

"And the buildings are kind of like sleek and kind of on pedestals," I began to explain. "They kind of appear and, then, disappear," I said matter-of-factly. "So really what you can see is the landscape, but once you look at a building, it appears. It's how they protect their environment. They're explaining it to me, but I don't quite understand what they're saying," I said. "But they're showing me it's kind of like how we park an electric car." I said, trying to establish a metaphor for what I was experiencing.

"Mm-hmm," Douglas responded as if he knew. I would become less surprised with Douglas's acceptances as we progressed through the series of hypnoses.

"They're on an energy field, so they appear when we need them," I explained. "And even when people are inside them, they disappear," I said and, then, trailed off. "They're cloaked. They're cloaked," I exclaimed, finally finding some understanding in the explanations. "So they have an energy field around them."

"So now you're talking about the buildings, right?" Douglas asked for clarification.

Douglas was right, but I was too excited with my new-found understanding. I ignored his request and kept talking.

"Like the word I keep hearing is titanium."

"Mm-hmm."

"Titanium," I said again as if I knew the significance of the word.

And, to be honest, on the other side, I *did* know the significance of many things. The spirit world always provided proof. From out of thin air, a set of technical drawings appeared, larger than they should have been, not connected to anyone or anything physical. I read them, understood them, and nodded my disinterest.

"There's something they're showing; they're telling me to pay attention," I said trying to narrate and seeking to understand the guidance all at the same time. "When you breathe in, it's like when you're in a sandstorm or when you're on the beach and the wind blows and you breathe some of it in," I said. "And that's left over from when they were developing; the scar is from when they were developing," I explained, but left unsaid the fact that the spirit beings intended me to understand that *when they were developing* was meant to convey a time when they were unsophisticated and low-intelligenced. Like humans are now. And when I finally did understand the comparison, I made a conscious choice not to say it. "They scarred the environment, but they're making it better," I finished.

While it had only been a number of minutes since I had entered the hypnotic state, I had spent hours and hours looking at the living image the spirit world had created, the living image of my home. The place of my first incarnation. As the colors and sounds, the smells and sites and people finally became normal, Michael appeared at my side; his radiance shone around and through me. *Protection,* I thought.

"Michael says it's time to go. I have work," I said.

I looked around nostalgically, and I thought back to the too many times I had had the same experience. So often I've stood somewhere—in the woods of Versailles as the sun dipped and the candle-lit lanterns were lighted, on the Indian Ocean as the blood moon shone in the sky, in a little frescoed church in the mountains of Cyprus, on Ireland's Cliffs of Moher—and wondered if I would ever see the places again. Even before I left, I felt a deep longing, almost homesickness for them. It was the same feeling that pumped through me as Michael moved me on from the image of my soul planet.

Will I see it again? I asked Michael.

Yes. And you will now notice the similarities that exist on earth.

In the time since the question to Michael, I *have* noticed similarities. On late summer evening walks with my little shitzu, I stand in front of a dusky Rocky Mountain sky of lilac and spidery orange shafts of light, and I think of home. Not my current home—earth, but my star home. And when I hear the droning buzz of a single engine plane that drags banners across the summer sky of ocean bathers, I feel a distant, eons-held memory reemerge. At least a little. This memory settles with the smell of a tiny spray of orange peel as it is separated from the fruit or with the heat lightning that silently slices through a starry night. They, too, remind me of what I once knew as home.

I have also noticed what is different. The sun. The blue of the sky. The clouds. I'm pretty sure the sun on my soul planet is further away, and so the bright light of earth is something I know from the in-between and not from my soul planet. Here on earth, I marvel at cotton candy clouds. Big ones and small ones and mere wisps of clouds cobbled together in lines across the sea of cerulean blue sky. Sometimes a hint of grey on moody mornings overlays the scene. Like sleepers in the corners of the sky's eyes, the grey represents a not-quite-ready-to-accept-the-sun sky. Like an anthropologist, I catalog these images for a later time—mind memories, I call them. Now I understand why.

"I'm where I was the other day on a high platform," I tell Douglas. "I've created it," I laughed. "There's nothing physical; it just feels like it's a platform. I see a podium. I see this structure I'm standing on with Michael, but it's just for me. It's just to make me feel comfortable," I tried to explain and, then, continued. "The light beings are here. In the same position."

"You're talking about The Twelve?" Douglas asked when the silence grew long.

"They're not here yet," I blurted out, but I didn't really mean what I had said and knew I had to refine my answer.

The Twelve were always there. Hovering. Waiting. Giving me the chance to absorb everything before they showed themselves.

"They only come in a little at a time for me. They're too much all at once," I said and, then, abruptly shifted focus. "My dad is here again. They bring my dad," I said, assuming Douglas would understand.

In my father's physical life, his mission was to ensure that my essence— joy—would be projected as a strength and not get mired in the denseness of the physical body. Joy, I understood, attracts darkness in the physical realm; there are forces that attempt to cudgel humanity through a misinterpretation of hate. They would work to dampen my spirit, my joy, my light. They would turn my joy against me, weakening me, causing me to fold up within myself so I did not seek out my mission, my path. But I had a job to do. An important one, the spirit world reminded me, and my father's mission focused my light. It wasn't an easy task for him and many times my love and enthusiasm and joie de vivre were dampened by an ugly reaction from the physical world. My father had been successful, however, and the spirit world now used his success and stability in my earth life to ease me into the transition from ego to messenger.

"Here comes the lilac. It's like a crystal. When I see them coming, it's like a crystal, but it's not a crystal," I said, the words quickening with anticipation. "It's like a fissure in the fabric of where we are," I explained.

As I awaited the arrival of The Twelve, I turned back to describing the setting in front of me. I landed first on the rows and rows of light beings—amorphously-shaped, but gloriously lit. Their spirit touch and mind communication were not restricted by their physical space. Instead, their warm breezy touch and simultaneous stories filled me with a sense of belonging, community, and a feeling of pure joy.

"The light beings are some kind of protection," I said. "They're in spirit. I don't want to say *army*, but if I were going to pick a word,

I'd say army. But there's no," I stopped to choose my words carefully. "Aggression," I finally said. "No aggression. Just a shared mission. A shared mission with us," I explained. "These are ours. These are ours. They are assigned to us."

Around and between and from within the spirit entities, a brilliant white light effervesced, its illumination like the spark from an overloaded old knob-and-tube wired plug. Like a sparkler, but infinitely brighter and more replicated to fill the alive emptiness of everything. Everything. It was lovely, pleasant, not at all harsh, despite its intensity. The light was animated, not static. It zipped and zapped and sizzled in the ether. Crystalline in nature, lines of barely visible snowflake-like structures, flittered, moved, tinkled in the no-air of the forum. If I were to draw a comparison, it would be to connect it with the kind of light I imagine surrounding me as I meditate. Divine white light, it is called in meditation circles.

"When I was a little girl, there was an amusement park, and it had a haunted house that was really lame," I laughed.

As was the case in the spirit world, my memories surrounding the haunted house reestablished themselves in my present. I relived the actual events, and because we are connected in the spirit world, I was able to access the feelings, emotions, and physical sensations of every other person involved. All the memories and each actor's emotions happened simultaneously, a multi-layered explosion of impression and perception. I focused on just one to feel it most intensely; I was young—the summer after sixth grade—and I felt all the growing angst of an almost-teenager bubbling up inside me. I had only recently begun to measure myself against the physical beauty of others, and I longed to reach out to the child I was to dissuade her from such comparisons. It would become a habit, I knew, a habit that would chip away at my confidence. I wanted her to ignore the gnawing sense of not enough.

Don't do this to yourself—to us, I pleaded with the young me.

She recognized my intrusion and ignored my message as she looked around for its source.

While I debated with the younger me, I also felt one brother's innocence, his innate naivete, and as I considered the life he would face, I prayed he could find a way to keep the innocence intact. It would help him survive the tests he would face in his life. My other brother felt the fear of the ride facing us; he was the youngest, the baby. All three of us were trapped in our human individuality unable to connect to each other in support as we might have done in the spirit world. We simply moved on, each of us harboring our own baggage. As tracks led the mechanized car into the Haunted House, I said good-bye to the young us and felt a pang of nostalgia. And, as this one memory came to an end, the other simultaneous scenes also folded like a house of cards in my mind.

"But we all liked it," I said of the haunted house. And we'd go on the car in the dark, and there was probably a mop hanging from the ceiling, and it would go across your head as you went underneath it. This light touch," I said moving my fingers to illustrate my point. "And that's what happens when I'm around them," I said sweeping my arm across the army of light beings standing guard in the spirit world.

"Around the light beings?" Douglas asked.

"Yeah. And their touch is familiar. There are so many, but I know each individual touch. It just brushes," I said, spending a few seconds of silence just feeling the touches. "The mood is lighter today," I said. "Some of them came quickly into form and, then, out," I said, referring to the light beings. "Directors," I heard them called by other spirit beings.

While I was preparing to explain what I meant by the directors, The Twelve entered, and my attention shifted to them. I never fully explained the new group to Douglas; instead, I thought I would return to the conversation a later in an effort to sharpen my explanation. But I couldn't remember what I needed to say about them after I emerged from hypnosis. In fact, I forgot most of my interactions with them. I did remember, however, that the members of the group—the directors—made soul contracts to enter physical bodies for one particular purpose. They were on a short-term lease, not for a whole human lifetime. Once they completed their mini-mission, they returned to the spirit realm. I had examples at the moment of the original narration, but afterwards, I had forgotten them completely. Especially as The Twelve stood illuminated in front of me.

"They're here," I said. "They're present."

Douglas registered his acknowledgement of my statement as if he already knew.

"Not all the archangels are here today, but a few," I narrated the changing scene. Unlike the formal entrance of the archangels during my last visit, this time, the archangels were entering, milling around, less ceremonial. "I don't know them all, but I can tell you one. Pink. Haniel. She's pink, or it looks like pink. The colors are different," I tried to explain. "She's different; she stands out because," I laughed in sympathy, "she's shorter than the other light columns. Instead of energy going up, hers goes out."

I stopped to look around and noticed another archangel. "Raphael, he's green. Deep green," I told Douglas. "He's powerful. I'm almost a little afraid of him," I said, my ego kicking in. "He's got a sense of majesty to him."

After a few minutes of thought, I tried to explain my fear, knowing full well that I was interpreting Raphael's regal way through the lens of a self-doubting earth being. "He projects like a very stern, no nonsense . . .," I trailed off as I noticed another angel. "Gabriel is in light blue. Sparkly though. And, for me, Gabriel comes as a man, but for most, Gabriel comes as a woman," I said. "And it's because the energy is more tender."

The angels—especially archangels—present in a form and/or gender that is most comforting to the viewer; it helps alleviate some of the fear that comes with awe. At least a little.

"There's a smoky one too," I said, after another archangel entered my consciousness. "I don't know who it is. Smoky. If I say he's all greys and blacks, I don't mean that to be negative in any way. That's just the color. It's as vibrant as the more vibrant-hued archangels." After a long silence, I continued, "They're powerful. But I can't figure out how to use the words right. They're powerful, but they're also servants. I just mean they're mission driven."

"What I would say is they're in service to the *All That Is*," Douglas tried to clarify for me.

While I had always had a connection to Michael and, sometimes, Gabriel, Douglas was actively *working* with the group as a whole. He knew them, therefore, much better than I did. My descriptions were not as new to him as they were to me.

"Yeah. And they're deeply connected," I said and trailed off. I knew Douglas knew what I meant, but Douglas prompted me to complete the thought.

"Deeply connected to?"

"Source."

"Yes," he agreed.

"And deeply protective of Source. They don't have to be, of course," I said and, then, struggled with how to clarify what I meant. "It's like a child who's protective of parents."

"Ah-hah. It comes from love," Douglas agreed.

"Yes. I like when they stand together because their lights mingle and change. There's an aura that comes off them. And they kind of temper Raphael a little bit," I laughed.

In response to my remark, Raphael turned to me, shook his head, and rolled his eyes as a parent might to mildly chastise a child. Of course, he had no head to shake; he had no eyes to roll. Yet, he made me *feel* as if he did so that I could interpret the gesture through my human experience. It was a joke between us. For me, this small interaction was a break-through. It made me feel less awe-full in his presence.

"But they are awed by The Twelve," I said referring to the archangels. "*Jasmine*," I whispered, seemingly unconnected to anything I was narrating. "I heard *Jasmine* when I said The Twelve. I'm supposed to look that name up. I think it's a flower."

"Mm-hmm," Douglas agreed. "And a smell."

"Yeah."

Later, when I *Googled* jasmine, I found a <u>*Gardening Tips | Flower Wiki*</u> entry. The author wrote: "the jasmine flower's message is mysteriously complex and means different things in different settings. Its pristine beauty and heady fragrance speaks of love and evokes positive feelings." The word comes from Persian, and I knew the name Yasmin /ياسمين/ from my time in the Middle East. Interested in the meaning of the word, I texted my Arabic-speaking husband in Dubai: "What does Yasmin mean in Arabic?" His response: "Gift from God."

"They said they'll be easier on me today," I laughed.

"See, there is mercy," Douglas joked.

"Yes," I laughed in response. "Mercy is one of their names."

"How interesting," Douglas said.

"Mercy is one of their names," I repeated. After a little silence, I translated a joke for Douglas, "they laugh that sometimes you follow your guidance."

"Despite myself."

"Right. Despite yourselves, they correct. You're incarnated somewhere else too," I tried to explain.

"Oh, I am?" Douglas asked, and once again, I was surprise by his *I-already-kinda-knew-that* response. "I didn't know I was this time. Somewhere else on this planet?"

"No," I answered uncharacteristically quickly.

"No," he agreed.

"You have a dual mission. They said they've spread you thin."

"Well, that sounds kind of rude," Douglas joked. He was beginning to interact with The Twelve.

"They think it's funny. They have so much majesty. So much awe. They make me feel so little. Not in a bad way; I don't mean that in a bad way."

"It's just so humbling," Douglas explained.

"Humbling," I whispered in agreement. "Oh, they're going to answer questions for *you*," I told Douglas; "so here's your first question that they're going to answer," I said.

Since Douglas had not asked a question, at least not out loud, I felt a little self-conscious telling him an answer was coming. The Twelve had heard his thoughts although, even if they hadn't, the question of the dual mission hung heavy in the room.

"I appreciate that," Douglas joked. "Pointing those things out."

"So you are Stellar. At the soul level," I began.

Stellar. It is a single, but it described a higher sentient being, one connected closely to Source, highly intelligent, and living in another star system. Stellar is a weighty word; it conveys stature on a physical being; they are so evolved, dimensional, linked.

"And you agreed to come here, but you're also part of the mission in your own star system," I continued. And you feed data from here. Like a computer almost."

"Ah-hah," Douglas responded, seeming to understand the far-reaching implications of his role. "So I'm on a mission as an Arcturian as well?"

"Yes," I answered although I had no idea what *Arcturian* meant. "And they have given you the ability to 'combine your halves' is what they're saying. I kind of think I know what they mean by it, but we have separate existences, and we're not usually aware of the other."

"Right," Douglas affirmed.

"But you've been given a gift. Of being able to unite. It's a hard mission, but this is also a gift. This is a gift for you for something you did in the past."

"And what would that be?" Douglas asked.

"Wait," I said.

In fact, the command was not meant for Douglas; instead, The Twelve had said it to me, and I thoughtlessly repeated it out loud. Because scenes and conversations and experiences happened simultaneously in the spirit realm, I was having trouble with completing one story before moving on to the next. I was relearning how to interact in the nonlinear aspect of the other side, and I wasn't good at it.

Finish, I was instructed; *this is important,* The Twelve told me.

"You brought awareness before for which they've given you the gift of bringing awareness with you now, especially into this dense of an existence," I explained. "And what did you do in the past?" I asked as I relived the moments from Douglas's past life.

There was darkness—an inky, almost absolute black—on a planet where the entire civilization had been destroyed, vaporized. As I searched the darkness, I could hear laughter and crying and conversations, the humming of a transportation system, the high-pitched screech of an animal. I heard the noise of daily life. Until I couldn't. Like snapping a finger, I could hear it, and then I couldn't. I relived the end of the civilization in those moments of sound.

Back in the present-past, the crystalline surface reminded me of anthracite coal: glassy-like at the cut; all rough and dull on its surface. Black. Very deeply black. There was a light source coming from a ship; a tractor beam of sorts shone on a lone being; she was laying on the ground, propped up on her right arm, her body heaving with sobs. Two beings stood looking from within; both had high positions. Both were wrangling with the choice they had made to leave her to die on the surface of a dead planet.

The only other structure was a landing site, raised up on a high platform, behind and slightly to the right of the being on the planet's surface. It was a flat silvery color, sleek and metallic, a lonely outpost left behind by those who had not survived a disaster that ultimately destroyed their planet. The result was a surface void of life and contour and structure. The black of the surface rose to meet the black of the night sky; only the stars provided relief to the infinity of blackness. And the light from the ship where the two beings stood.

I felt the conflict of the two in the ship. The woman on the surface was a comrade, a shipmate, a friend. I understood what would happen; I already knew it. Felt it. Lived it. But I felt the inner tension of both characters as they made their separate decisions.

"Someone was being left behind," I said sadly, clearly affected by what I was viewing. "I feel it was a virus or something. Someone was being left behind," I said again, focusing on the drama of the moment. "You had to," I said directly to Douglas.

I understood that while one life had merit, misplaced mercy could potentially cost the lives of all the others. The two leaders had to make an agonizing decision to trade that one life for the well-being of all the others. The thin, poisonous air, they had calculated, would result in a quick death for the being. Or, a relatively quick death. Together with the virus, they believed the being would last three days. Maybe four. She would succumb to an oxygen-deprived sleep, her limbs limp and unmoving. Alone. An eternally, lonely fixture on the surface of the anthracite planet.

It was a decision that reminded me of the kind made by oxygen-deprived hikers on Everest. One hiker, racked with mountain sickness and the inability to move forward, would be left to die so that the others had a chance to live. An agonizing decision that forces those who decide to measure another's worth as a living being.

"And you stayed," I finally had the courage to tell Douglas. "And in this existence, they had both genders. You were complete in one," I explained the frivolous detail to avoid the end I was experiencing in the drama I was living: the one left behind and the one who stayed. "And you stayed. I will say *she*, but it's both. *She* died in your arms."

"Mmm-hmm," Douglas sighed.

"And you died alone. It was not your mission," I explained. Your mission was finished, and it would have been easy," I explained.

"Was I Arcturian in this life?" Douglas asked.

"No. Close. Your soul's base is Arcturian. This was close. Arcturians are not two genders," I said as if the explanation were obvious.

"Can they tell me do I know this being that I stayed for? Is this being in my life today?" Douglas asked.

"Yes," I answered quickly. "But not here."

Hmm.

"But you know."

"I do, huh?" Douglas asked.

"Yes. That's why he keeps an eye on you. It's the tall one."

"Golodor?"

"Yes."

"Mmm."

"And because of that selflessness," I continued, "did you know that . . .," I trailed off.

"No," Douglas answered, but it was an answer to another question.

"Did you know that," I restarted, "many Stellars know their mission almost intuitively? Follow it. Finish it. And then know. Know they're finished their mission, and then it's almost like a vacation. And you knew. You knew you were done your mission," I said, returning to the lonely drama on the ruined planet. "And you stayed. You extended yourself. You didn't change the mission of the other person. You just showed compassion. And so your gift was to come back with awareness. Even to this existence. And this earth one is the hard one . . . the hard one to maintain an awareness on."

"You mean this one on earth?" Douglas asked for clarification.

"Yes. So when you think you're standing somewhere else, it's your other half. It's a check in. A uniting of your soul parts."

After a few minutes of discussing the tragic scene with Golodor, I added, "he's tall. Golodor is tall. I keep calling him Gandalf because that's who he reminds me of," I said, referring to the wizard in the *Lord of the Rings* movies. "And his neck feels very long to me," I explained. "He has awareness, too. He knows," I said. "He knows."

"So, let me just get this straight," Douglas interrupted; "Golodor is a manifestation of that being that I stayed for?"

"Yes."

"Okay."

"But many lives in between," I said.

"No, I got that. Okay. And I have a parallel . . ."

57

As he spoke, I was taken back to the anthracite planet. After the first being died, the past manifestation of Douglas built a monument of black stones around her body. The building distracted him from the sense of alone-ness that grew in him. He had only a single light source, and he used it like the light on an iPhone to keep track of time. The blackness had made it almost impossible, yet he worked to structure the time he had left so that he didn't succumb to self-pity and desperation. Instead, he engaged in a kind of meditation where he relived the happy moments of his lives. Almost seven days after his decision to stay, he surrendered his life. Seven days is a long time for some things. His body remains on the black planet propped up against the monument he built for the other.

"There are many lives together that you shared together," I told Douglas.

"But I also have a parallel life? And that parallel life is as an Arcturian?"

"Yes."

"Okay. And?"

"So's Golodor," I interrupted again.

"Yeah, and he's also on my soul council?"

"No. Council of Elders," I explained. "For Arcturians."

"Okay," Douglas breathed out his understanding. "Now I'm getting it."

"He's high. Hierarchy. Not like here, but he is an honored being."

"Mm-hmm."

"And his seat . . . for Arcturus? His seat for Arcturus is a seat on the council with the Federation."

"Yes, okay," Douglas said. "So, he's the representative from Arcturus to the Federation?"

"Yes. One," I answered and, then, clarified, "Of two."

"Mm-hmm."

"Your soul council is different," I said as if it were obvious, as if everyone knew.

"Yes. And that's what I misunderstood when you said *Council of Elders* last time. I mistook that.'

"There are five," I said raising my hand, spreading my fingers for Douglas to see.

"On my Council of Elders?"

"No."

"No. On the Arcturian council."

"No. On your *Soul Council*," I tried to explain. "When we go between lives ...."

"Mm-hmm," Douglas interrupted.

"And they cleanse you. Maybe debrief you a little. And they're a hard group," I offered. "You have them because you can take them. Some cannot."

As I finished the narrative of the anthracite planet, I was reminded that I had not fully explained the roll of the light beings that stood at the ready—an army of non-aggressors. *Finish*, I was reminded, and although it had seemed ages since I had moved from that particular scene, the scene reestablished itself in my psyche so that I could explain it adequately for Douglas.

This is important, I heard, and I knew that a transition would soon be made.

"Some of the light beings here today are beings that you lived lives with before. You have a soul pact with them. They need to help. Most of their soul is still part of the in-between," I tried to explain. "Some are for me. But all of them are for us to help us succeed," I explained.

"But don't feel any pressure, right?" Douglas joked when he felt my mood sour a bit.

"I don't feel pressure," I laughed. "They're funny today."

"I know," Douglas laughed, but he had succeeded in allaying the fear of my ego. "It's just what my mind did with it: *you should be really nervous!*" he joked

"It feels like so much less pressure than the last time. It feels lighter."

"Right."

As I said it, I remembered Douglas asked for more fun in the first session, and I had the sense that he was being granted his request.

"Everyone feels like they're smiling today. They weren't so happy the other day."

"Yeah," Douglas said with a sigh.

"We can call on them, the light beings" I said. "We've interacted with them on the earth in short bursts. They manifested into a physical body quickly and disappeared quickly. They call themselves *Directors*. Almost like spiritual guides, but in physical form. A brief physical form."

"That explains a few experiences I've had," Douglas replied.

"Yes. They showed me you looking at weather reports. Or in papers, reading weather reports. I don't know why they're telling me, but it's apparently something you're supposed to transmit: the weather reports."

"Am I?" Douglas asked about the weather reports.

"Yes, and . . .."

"I don't read weather reports," Douglas responded.

"Oh, but you do," I responded as if I knew better than he.

"Oh, okay," Douglas conceded.

"That's an important part of your daily transmission. This information is important to the Stellars. Stellars are physical entities," I felt compelled to explain.

"Mm-hmm."

"But they have a high vibration. And a high intellect. And they are able to break the boundary between physical existence and the spiritual. Not always, but often. And they benefit from that," I explained although I knew the greater soul voice of The Twelve had begun to take over. "There's not supposed to be boundaries between the physical and spirit world."

A Message from The Twelve: Jasmine and the Beginning of the Story

A long silence ensued as the physical me was sent off on a mission, and The Twelve took over the conversation with Douglas. While it was my voice that Douglas heard, my earth psyche was busy talking to the army of light warriors in the spirit world. Because it was such an important mission, they would be activated to help spread the message, and their involvement would sustain me in the hard times ahead. Although I knew my conversation with the army of light workers was significant, I had the distinct feeling I had been sent to occupy my ego elsewhere, so the message could be voiced without interruptions. Even so, I was able to participate in the conversation with Douglas and The Twelve, just not so actively.

Out of the millions of layers of soul voices that made up The Twelve, one voice emerged as the dominant one. I still heard the beautiful cacophony of souls, but they became the back-up band to the strong melody of a single resonant voice that spoke through my physical being. She was me. Or rather I was part of her. She was one of The Twelve, the one that radiated a joy vibration. My soul was part of her eternity. I understood that my full, between-life soul was housed in the individual voice, and it comforted me like a mother's voice soothes her frightened child. It also triggered me. Knowledge flooded through and around and into my awareness; I knew what she knew. I saw what she saw. I experienced what she experienced, and

I remembered the many, many lives we had lived over our many millennia of existence. Because she held it all, the earth me was not overwhelmed, and I knew I would relinquish it all—or most of it—when I reemerged from hypnosis.

"The Stellars are the light. They're light beings. There are some Stellars that have lost their light." She called these lost light beings Astrals to distinguish them from other Stellars. "And Astrals walk among us here on earth," the voice continued. "They seem to have lost their spirit, their soul. It's there. But it's buried so deep, they feel like shells. They are physical beings only," a much more controlled, much more modulated voice, a voice of authority and knowledge said.

"Are they in physical form?" Douglas asked.

"Yes."

"Yeah."

"And they seek us out," the spirit voice said, using *us* to refer to humanity.

"Hmm," Douglas added, understanding the gravity of the conversation.

"And we know them," she continued. "We can feel the heaviness when they come by us."

In my mind, I had a flash of faces. They were young and old, sweet and not, longing and probing and lost. Each time I came face to face with a memory of what the soul voice called Astrals, I remembered the way they looked at me—a sideways glance, through squinted eyes, peripherally and expectant. I felt their condescension in a glare. I caught a whiff of their contempt. I had always interpreted our interactions through a swarm of my earthly insecurities. Now I understood my intuition was giving me necessary guidance. *Stay away*, it said, but I didn't always listen to it. I never wanted to be cruel or unkind, so I often paid a steep price for this misplaced counsel of mine.

When I was in college, for example, I joined the crew team and became the bow in an eight-woman boat. I had never rowed before. Not ever. But I took to it. The early, early morning practices began before the sun rose; as we pulled oars through grey water to warm up, our minds were engaged in the work and not our surroundings. As we finished and our attention was redirected outward, we recognized how we had become one with the awesome morning ritual taking place all around us. The sun had just begun to peek over the horizon, and the steam of our bodies synced with the early morning haze on the river. Our warm breath competed with the cold of dawn, and fresh found its way in as we pulled our oars and pulled in air. Small assemblies of mallards quack, quack, quacked on the surface, and the landscape slowly emerged from the obscurity of night's black. My boatmates and I had lost our individuality during our warm-up; it had been worked out of us, and a kind of synergy took over. Swing, we called it in crew. Lines of orangey-golden light zig-zagged through the water, and our oars slapped and splashed the surface interrupting their paths. The sky lightened little by little from gray to lilac to deep blue as the sun began its ascent. They were glorious mornings when all was right with the world. Although I didn't know how to call it consciously at the time, the combination of work and cold and beauty and collaboration raised my natural joy vibration, the vibration that radiated from my greater soul.

Not everyone resonated with my joy on those mornings, however. Our coxswain was a small, slender, pretty thing who seemed virtually empty of any feeling whatsoever. Her brains and beauty camouflaged her deficiencies. She was colder than the early morning March air. She neither smiled nor laughed although the banter in the boat would provide plenty of opportunity for both. She did not like me. "Nobody's that happy," she'd say behind my back. I tried to work with her, to be friends with her, but she simply stared at me through blank eyes, and in the end, I grew to fear her.

In one particularly memorable moment from my life, I saw our coxswain at a party. She stood in the middle of the room dressed in a beautiful black cashmere dress. She was alone in a crowd, a satellite that cleared space around her as she moved. When I entered the room, our eyes met, and like a scene from a B movie, the distance between us collapsed into nothing although we never physically moved towards each other. A cold sweat worked itself up my spine, and I tingled with the feel of pins and needles. When the tractor beam of our gaze was finally broken, I shivered with new knowledge. I knew—I just *knew*—she was not what she seemed, and afterwards, kept my distance physically, emotionally, and psychically. As my greater soul spoke to Douglas, the story of the coxswain finally made sense.

"The coldness," she continued. "They seem convivial and happy and people we want to be friends with, and they connect to us. But we realize, fairly quickly, who they are. We see the undercurrent. We feel it. We feel their emptiness."

My ego returned to the conversation between Douglas and my greater soul. As I heard her words, I was only just coming to terms with the Astrals I had known in my life. I wanted to understand why I continued to try with them despite the warning I received from guidance. *I* felt guilty that the coxswain didn't like me, for example. So I interpreted my greater soul's words to assuage my own faults.

"We've attempted to save them—the Astrals," I said; "and I'm embarrassed by the word save."

"Mm-hmm," Douglas noted the re-emergence of my ego.

"And they're telling me the intention is fine. They don't judge us. They don't judge me," I said before submitting, once again.

You must allow me to explain, the spirit voice told me.

Who are you? I asked.

You are part of me, she answered. *Together, we make up a whole soul.*

What's your name? was all I could think to ask.

Jasmine. You can call me Jasmine.

"But there are many more Astrals now than there were before," Jasmine continued.

"And why is that?" Douglas interrupted after a long silence.

"Because, for a while, we were moving in the right direction. Because humanity is fundamentally a joy vibration. That was our role. We were conceived as the joy vibration. That's why I'm here," Jasmine explained.

"When you say *we*, are we talking about *Akia*?" Douglas asked referring to my soul name.

"Yes. You remembered."

"I did. Sometimes names are important," Douglas said.

"That brought sunshine," she said after a long silence.

For some reason, hearing my soul name calmed me. Coming from Douglas, it sounded funny. He could not imitate the tone that was part of the name, and his vowels were a little off, but he managed it as well as he could in English and that had an impact on the physical me. It made me smile. In the spirit world, such joy emanated brighter than our sun.

After a few more seconds, Jasmine picked up the original topic: "Because we emanate joy as the basis of who we are—as humans, we link. It's why a racist can say terrible things one day and help his black neighbor the next day. Because our compulsion is to link, to be part of each other. But the Astrals are shells; they have lost their light. It's there," Jasmine felt compelled to clarify. "It's there, but it's lost on the surface. They don't act on it anymore."

"I'm sorry," Douglas interjected. "Their light is not on the surface? Is that what you said?"

"Yes."

"Okay."

"Their light is inside so deep that we don't see it as there. It's there. So they have increased in numbers to create division on earth. They need to keep us apart," Jasmine warned. "But you can see what happens," she said, her voice rising in hope. "It's a funny thing—the human species. So many who would have chosen to be neutral before, have chosen the path of acceptance and linking. They understand. But there are too many who don't. These Astrals have created a compulsion to link within their sphere. They figured out that humanity, at its core, links in joy, so they've created an alternative. They link in hate. And in a funny way, the hate is a joyous thing for the group."

"For the group that links in hate?" Douglas asked.

"Yes."

"Yeah."

"They," she said meaning humans, "still fundamentally find the joy despite the fact that they link in hate. Their light is still there too. They've been manipulated. It's not political leaders that create this."

"Some political?" Douglas asked, having missed the first part of the sentence.

"It is *not* political leaders that create this."

"Right."

"They take advantage of it. They, too, are manipulated."

"Yeah," Douglas sighed. "They don't know that."

"They do not," Jasmine said sadly. "But the more they manipulate it, the more it empowers the hate and the more joy that comes from hate. The message—part of the message—is that joy comes from *linking*, not from the hate."

When Jasmine spoke, there was a clear delineation between my own voice and the cadence, rhythm, and control of her voice. It resided in a different world without time, without concern. Silence was okay; in fact, it was wise as Douglas processed the new information. Jasmine was more confident than me, knew what she wanted to say, and had far fewer hedges in her communication style.

"Humanity faces its end," Jasmine warned. She allowed her pronouncement to hang in the air.

"Because of the hate?" Douglas asked after a very long silence.

"Because of the manipulation. They will destroy themselves," she added, clearly meaning humanity.

"And the manipulation is essentially being driven by the darkness?" Douglas asked.

"Yes. From the Astrals."

"Yeah. So the Astrals are representatives of darkness? Or are they just our darkness?"

"No. There is no darkness. There's just choice. There's only Source. But the Astrals separated themselves for so long from Source, the believe their own story. And this, in earth terms, creates darkness. You've seen the joy in the faces of the hate. The haters."

As Jasmine spoke, my mind filled with images of the Nazi-like display in Charlottesville, Virginia, in 2017. She spoke to me softly as she tried to re-focus my ego; at the same time, she talked to Douglas.

"She sees Charlottesville in her mind, and she's right," Jasmine tells Douglas. "She sees the happiness they felt when they stood together and said hateful things. It's not the *hate.*"

"It's the linking, huh?" Douglas adds.

"It's the linking that brings them joy.

"But the manipulation is to believe it's the hate, "Douglas said.

"Yes. Yes. It's obvious."

"And that's part of the message?"

"Yes," Jasmine answered. "It's so obvious. It's so obvious. So many signs. We've given so many; they're like beacons," she said. "The beacon emits the vibration of joy again, reminding people it's the joy of linking that creates it. The day Notre Dame burned. Do you remember?" Jasmine asked Douglas. Do you remember?"

"Mm-hmm."

"And watching the people on the street. Some of the same people could have watched someone murdered and stepped over the body, but the beacon emitted a vibration, and they remembered. And they stood together linked in a common cause." After a long pause as she waited for a question from Douglas, Jasmine continued with another example, "Even New York after 9/11. Do you remember?" she asked. "Do you remember the feeling of *Wow. This is New York; look at the people stand together?"*

"Mm-hmm."

"It was the joy of being linked to one another," she said. "They forget."

"What is it that they forget?"

"They forget the simple joys: the holding of a child's hand," Jasmine said. "The face of an older parent; the touch of their partners," she added. "Every day joy in linking given to them. Every day they hear this story. Every day they understand, but they don't translate it to the bigger world."

As she explained the concept to Douglas, I relived my own memory of my infant son, just home from the hospital, his toddler sister sitting next to me. I felt Katlyn's joy and confusion as she confronted the new member of our family. I smelled Collin's baby-powder clean and experienced the joy of kissing his tiny foot. It was a moment so ordinary, yet in reliving it, I understood the moment as profound. The three of us sat together linked in joy. We expressed love in the extraordinary ordinariness of the moment, and we felt no daylight between us. We were safe. We were connected, not just by familial ties, but through joy, and we emanated that joy throughout the universe. In other words, the joy we emitted filtered through our world and out into the universe, and we were, through the simple act of linking, living the mission that humans were created to live.

"Hatred is the weed that has been planted in your garden," Jasmine said.

"I'm sorry; I didn't hear the beginning of the sentence," Douglas responded.

"Hatred is a weed."

"Okay."

"It is a beautiful world," she said after another long silence.

As she spoke to Douglas, she carried me throughout the world to see our favorite places. I showed her the savannah of Kenya, the lions roaring, the wildebeest splashing at the water's edge, a herd of zebras zig-zagging as one across the plains; she showed me the tundra of Alaska and pointed out the purples and pinks of the light show in the night sky. I showed her the water of the Indian Ocean where villagers carried nets to wooden boats for the day's catch; she took me to the desert sands of the Empty Quarter where the imprints of camel's hooves marked the dunes where the sun began its descent. We were not competing with each other; instead, we stood together in admiration of such beauty.

I like to experience earth, she told me.

I nodded. I, too, had been captured by the beauty I had seen in my travels.

It is lonely," Jasmine said, reading my thoughts. *Because we are not from this planet, but the changing colors and varied seasons and natural beauty bring me back.*

Again, I nodded my agreement, and she smiled. We shared the same soul. I was her; she was me. A little part had been cleaved from her vast soul and placed in a physical manifestation—me—to gather life experiences.

But it is not all about experiences, she warned. *You have a mission.*

"She likes the ocean," she told Douglas of our travels together; "but I like the night sky over the desert. Quite a masterpiece."

With the passion in Jasmine's words, I understood, for the first time, why I was compelled to live in the Middle East. It was a wish of my greater soul to live in that beauty, and after all, four years in an eternity of years is a small sacrifice for the greater good of the soul's longing. Moreover, I needed to experience being the *other* so that, when the time came, I would be able to recognize it and use the coping skills I had developed through such experiences in my physical manifestation.

"Do you have a question?" Jasmine asked after a very long silence.

"Probably," Douglas answered.

"Many, I think," she said.

"Well, you know how my mind goes too fast," Douglas said, searching for the right one.

"It's okay."

"I'm trying to link things together," he explained his hesitancy. "The Astrals you speak of, they have been born here? They are incarnated beings?"

"Mm-hmm."

"But these are the beings that have been drawn to be involved in the cabal?"

"Yes," Jasmine said, clearly amused by the word *cabal*.

"Okay."

"They also procreated here," she added.

"Mm-hmm. And when they procreate, do they create Astrals then?"

"Both."

"I'm sorry?"

"Both."

"Both," Douglas said, assessing his next line of questioning. "So sometimes they create people that have a full range of light?"

"Do you know the concept of *prima nocte*?

"I do not."

"The kings used to believe that when they take over a land, they would sleep the first night with a new wife," Jasmine explained. "They would breed disobedience out of the land. This is the idea."

As she spoke to Douglas, she explained to me that the concept was brought to the earth, not conceived on the earth. The Astrals, she said, had been doing it for generations: sleeping with earth women. Some tuned-in humans and the children of Astrals began to replicate the concept themselves. *It bred hate,* she explained. *And one's identity—a king or a peasant—manifested the hate in reference to the other.*

"Well, that helps me understand some things," Douglas sighed. "Because I always thought it was totally a free will choice, but I'm understanding that children of Astrals are most likely to be Astrals."

"No. Children of Astrals have free will, but most children love their parents."

"What an interesting paradox," Douglas began, "giving that we are talking about beings who have so much trouble with love, yet it's their love that has them become like their parents."

"It may work in the other direction as well. The parent's love may become the thing that moves the Astral."

"Okay. I've been wondering about that."

"Yes. The light is there."

"You're helping me understand how these people who can step over lots of bodies without flinching can," Douglas began, "have incredible feelings and attachment to their children and be protective parents. And I couldn't figure out if it was an act or the real thing."

"When we share our existence with another being that we helped create, it's powerful," she said. "Like when Source creates souls, it's a powerful pull on the new soul," she explained. "It's the same. It's replicated in the physical world."

"So do some of those Astrals actually discover that they have light inside them?" Douglas asked, seeking to clarify his own beliefs about the topic.

"Yes," Jasmine replied.

"And what do they do with that dissonance?"

"Forget. They forget their past when they walk away."

"Really?" Douglas asked surprised. "And so I'm assuming that there are some examples that are very known."

"A metaphor would be to think of gangs."

"Okay," Douglas said.

"Some get stuck inside," Jasmine explained, "and continue to do the will of the group because they're too weak to move away, but they know about the light," she said. "And it is these people who have potential to follow the message. They are divided."

"I'm sorry; you jumped. *These people* refer to?" Douglas asked.

"Those Astrals that . . . yes, a nice earth word would be . . . are *woke*. Those Astrals that know—that recognize their light. Some are strong enough to walk away," she explained. "Some are not," she added. "and continue to do the will of the group. But *they*," Jasmine emphasized, "have divided loyalties. If they could see a way, they would leave."

"Well, it would be my understanding that, like a gang, if you are identified with having divided loyalties, it could well cost you your life."

"Yes," Jasmine responded. "Yes. Yes."

"Given their belief about no light, there's nothing after the light."

"They believe in light," Jasmine corrected. "They believe they're right. They believe their light is showing them the right way. See? They do not believe—the group—they do not believe they do the wrong thing. They have built their story."

"And so, they cannot see that what they perceive as light is not?" Douglas asked.

"Right."

"Got it."

"Look for the examples of it playing out throughout the world. Look to the simple example of political parties."

"Mm-hmm," Douglas agreed.

"A foolish thing to connect with," Jasmine explained. "Again, that identifying agent of a political party has missed the point. The linking with other *beings* is joy. And in that link, there's not an *other*. We don't measure our joy by somebody's pain."

"So the linking vis a vis say a political party has been hijacked?"

"Yes. By the same. By the Astrals. Do you see?"

"Yes," Douglas agreed.

"You see the ideology coming through."

"Yes."

"Yes. All over you'll see evidence of this ideology filtering through. Even within families, you can see the ideology."

"I'm not conversant with the word *ideology*. Can you give me an example so I can thread it through?" Douglas asked.

"The ideology of the Astrals. The philosophy. The beliefs. The story they've written for themselves. The story, they believe, is the right story, and so they want people to listen to and agree with their story, and they've been effective. Identification, loyalties to some identifying source or some other ideology is ripe for that, for the sharing of their own story."

"So, let me just stay with this for a minute. So you have a group of Astrals who will present a certain way in a certain venue because it suits what they want, want they need?"

"It's who they are."

"They just become that. They're chameleons."

"Yes."

"Okay. So . . .."

"This is a good metaphor."

"Okay. I'm writing it down," Douglas joked. "Now my understanding that in private when they're together, they laugh at us. They laugh at us talking about love, talking about compassion. Help me; thread that through for me in terms of your story, your ideology piece."

"Well, their story is linking through hate."

"Hmm. Okay."

"Yes? They believe this. With hate comes the *other*. Do you see?"

"Mm-hmm."

"You have to have the others to have hate. That's why a child of theirs— even to one of the *others*, to one of the earth beings—creates confusion. Do you see? And so their story is linking through hate. And they find a pliable population in the *other*. They don't care about humanity. There's nothing they desire other than a type of slavery. A slavish connection to the story they craft. This gives them power. Acolytes. You see?"

"Mm-hmm," Douglas replied. "Accolades amongst themselves?"

"Aco*lytes*," she corrected.

"Aco . . . oh," Douglas understood. "Okay."

"Acolytes. Even earthly institutions use the story. The story has been changing humanity for millennia. It's not new," she explained.

"No."

"But it's at a zenith now."

"It most certainly is," Douglas agreed.

"For a long time, we let it evolve. And the Stellars let it evolve because of the gift of free will."

"And?" Douglas prodded after a long silence.

"And we are here, and there has been debate about our interruption. But not at the soul level," she explained the interruption; "at the physical level. What I say now might offend, but it just is," she warned Douglas. "Humanity has not evolved. It's been slow at evolving. It does not accept help. It shuns the Astrals," she said, and then corrected herself, "It shuns the Stellars and accepts the Astrals. It's not all their own fault, but at the physical level, we have made the decision to tell the message. To make it clear. And then? It's theirs."

"And this is part of what will go into the book?" Douglas asked.

"Yes."

"The Astrals will not like that," Douglas teased.

"The Astrals are not aware."

"They will be if there's a book."

"The Astrals will not know."

"It doesn't fit their story, huh?" Douglas asked.

"Their story does not permit this book. They might be aware of it, find it, and joke about it, but there are messages coming in different ways throughout the world. They may not seek out knowledge of the other side, and they would be particularly loathe to seek knowledge from the *other*, from a human."

"Do the Astrals know they're Astrals?" Douglas asked.

"Yes. Most," Jasmine replied. "Children, no. Not all."

"Children know they are or they identify them?"

"No, they don't know."

"Okay."

"Most don't know. It creates problems for the children. They are divided from their nature of joy and of the story that their own parent tells them. It creates conflict. You've seen these children. Empty."

"I have," Douglas admitted. "I have not treated them successfully, but I certainly have seen them."

"The Astrals are not the only ones who are here. The Stellars, too, come."

"And they, too, have been born on the planet?"

"Yes."

"And would you consider me one of those?"

"No. Your soul birth is Stellar. But you inhabit a physical body. Full. You understand the other side though because you twin. Because you unite with a Stellar," she explained, referring to the earlier conversation about Douglas's other incarnation.

After a few moments of silence, Jasmine told me it was time to go.

No, I said.

It is too much, she replied. *It is time.*

"Michael is here. He will escort her back," she told Douglas

Although I struggled a bit to stay, she used glimpses of my future to bring me back. *Go,* she told me. *Experience. Live.* As Michael warmed me in his light, I turned my back on the spirit world for just a fraction of a second, and in that time, I was through the door and on my way down the floating steps to home. My temporary home. The beautiful, vibrant, crazy earth. As I opened my eyes, disoriented and unclear, Douglas welcomed me back.

"Greetings," he said.

"How very Stellar of you," I replied.

ACT III

Fireflies

4 June 2019

Some souls cannot be confined to a particular place.
They are vast as the sky and deep as the ocean!
Avijeet Das

A Seer of Spirits; A Seeker of Truth

> We are souls, eternal and perfect, captains of our
> mystic ships: gods and goddesses of our universe.
> We are beautiful, we pearls of grit. We, the ember
> of everything. Our uniqueness IS what makes us
> special, and the expression of it is our gift to the rest
> of us. In order to feel happy and fulfilled, we must
> honour our own personal brand of creativity . . . let it
> out into the world . . . BE who we came here to BE.
> ~Angie Karan

As a young child, I was able to see and hear spirit. When I washed my face in the basin and lifted my head to the mirror hanging over it, I often saw another face looking back at me, a stranger's face, not mine. In the car with my parents and siblings, I positioned myself away from the rearview mirror, so I wouldn't see another's face peering back at me from the front seat. And when I walked over puddles or dove into water, I closed my eyes to avoid the reflection of spirits all around me. *All* around me. While I might feel rattled by the sudden appearance of spirit beings, I was not afraid of them. On the other hand, I didn't know how to explain them to the majority who didn't see them. The real fear came from being different, *too* different. Everyone— child or adult—has the need for community, and I didn't want to threaten mine by being a seer.

The fear of being found out was etched deep into my DNA. I had been outed before in other lives, in other physical manifestations, and I acted on the fear of the past in *this* physical manifestation by beginning a lifelong march towards left-brain activity. I went to school and gathered degrees; then, I used my education to research and write about respectable issues: equality in education, best practices for teaching children with special needs, and education for second language learners. Eventually, I became more comfortable speaking and living in an academic vernacular, so the right-brained connection to spirit became a thing of the past.

But it is impossible to hide such a gift away forever. It is just too big. Moreover, spirit have a way of showing up at the exact right moment. In times of need. As gifts from Source, the Divine, the Creator. In those moments, being a seer no longer marks difference but connotes comfort. When the gift is finally acknowledged and accepted, worlds align. Just like when towards the end of my second trimester as I carried my first baby, I experienced the most consistently intense pain of my life. *Something's wrong,* I thought. Dread ate at me. But by the next morning, the doctor reassured me: "I don't see any problems," he said. I felt relief—not from the pain, but from the panic that had creeped its way into my heart and mind. *Everything is just fine,* I repeated to myself over and over again, and I almost believed it was true. Until it wasn't. By midafternoon, I was in labor, working to deliver a baby boy who had already died.

In the evening when a natural delivery looked hopeless, the doctor explained the next step: an operation, an abortion. "There is no other way," she soothed as best she could while nurses wrapped me, cocoon-like, in a warming blanket. I wept. The tears pooled at my neck, my bound arms unable to wipe them away.

"Why are you crying?" a young nurse asked.

"No one will ever know him except me," I replied. "Like he never existed."

"But he did," she said.

"But no one else knows."

"You know," she comforted, wiping away the tears and crawling up on the table next to me. "He'll live through you."

The anesthesiologist interrupted our conversation as he prepared the drip, "when I put the medicine in," he motioned to the IV, "you will count backwards from ten, okay?"

"No," I whined.

The nurse answered by holding me—spooning me, really. She hummed in my ear and comforted me as I counted, slowly drifting off. I awoke in recovery, her melody easing me into full wakefulness, to the reality of my devastatingly raw and painful situation.

"Where is the nurse who held me on the operating table?" I asked.

"What nurse?"

"With the brown hair and green eyes. She laid on the table with me."

"Sweetie," the nurse began, pushing the hair from my eyes, "there was no nurse on the table. We were busy doing our jobs."

"You're wrong," I answered. "We spoke. She hummed in my ear."

"No, sweetheart. It was the anesthesia."

"He saw her," I blurted out. "The anesthesiologist. He saw her. Ask him," I begged.

She did; the anesthesiologist had not seen the nurse, but for weeks, I continued my quest to find her. I asked the supervisor, checked with my own doctor, and wrote letters to hospital administration. Their answers were always the same: there was no nurse. Except there was, and her song continued to pulsate through me, moving in my veins from heart to head and back again.

Almost two years later, after the birth of my beautiful daughter, I walked into a little arcade of specialty stores in an area of town I rarely, if ever, visited. As soon as I entered, I heard the familiar, haunting melody of the song—her song, the nurse's song—playing in one of the little specialty stores, *Somewhere in Time.*

"What's the name of this song?" I pleaded with the woman behind the counter. Her sad smile said she understood more than I could know.

"You lost someone?" she asked carefully.

Red rose through my cheeks, coloring my face. *How could she know?*

"You're not alone," she explained softly. "Someone hummed it to me as I waited. An operation. My daughter," she choked out. Then, sweeping her arm around the store, "that's why I opened this."

"My baby boy," I responded to her story, tears surging.

"She hummed this to you?" she asked, motioning to the music ceaselessly, endlessly playing in the background.

"Yes."

"And?" she asked.

"And there was no nurse," I replied. "She wasn't real."

She smiled, patted my hand, and moved around the counter to hug me. "Oh, she was there. She was real," she soothed.

I cannot describe the owner, what she looked like, how old she was, what she wore. I do not remember what she sold in the store or a single detail of what the store looked like. I do not know if the store is still open; I have never once returned. What I do know, however, is that I left that day with understanding, peace. I had finally found her. A profound spirit force—an emissary from God, the Creator, the Divine—had comforted me in a time of great need.

As I grew into adulthood, I learned to be cautious with what was considered normal in society. When I felt very comfortable with someone, I might break my silence or, at the very least, use my gift as a kind of parlor trick. I might read Tarot, for example, or recite poetry while the spirit-poet, himself, whispered the words to me. As I became more confident and the world opened up a bit more to the possibilities of communication with the spirit realm, I began to allow the gift to emerge fully, and I used it to soothe

the hearts of people burdened with loss. With each new step, I got closer and closer to my path, to finding Douglas and, through him, The Twelve. As I look back on the road that led me to his office, I can see the myriad signposts all along the way. A book. A teacher. A meditation group. A medium at a local Renaissance faire. A friend's father in spirit who helped me believe. A green-eyed nurse of comfort.

The Third Hypnotic Session: The Oneness of All in Source

"Open the door. Step through," Douglas said as he regressed me into hypnosis. "Close the door behind you and move into your personal sacred space," he instructed. "And whenever you're ready, just fill me in on what's going on," Douglas's voice called to me as I crossed the threshold into the spirit world.

For a long time after I arrived, I fought the impulse to narrate. I knew I had to, but I didn't want to. Douglas was waiting patiently for my narrative to begin, but more than a minute and a half went by before I whispered my first words, "Oh, it's the most amazing thing," I said and, then, stopped again for another long silence.

I had spent the countdown on the floating stairs with Archangel Michael, and for the first time, Archangel Gabriel joined us too. The latter archangel was hilarious, especially in comparison to the former's rigid seriousness. While Michael's radiance stood stiff, tall, Gabriel's bent wildly, spraying light everywhere like a flashlight turned on, tossing and turning and bouncing on the back seat of a beat-up old bus bumping its way over railroad tracks. The bright blue-lighted Gabriel made me laugh; in fact, he was so much fun I wanted to experience the moment, not recount it.

You must speak, the spirits said.

I don't want to. I had the sense of being a stubborn, petulant child.

It is your mission, they reminded me.

"I know them all," I said almost another minute later.

As I tumbled from the floating stairs into my sacred space in the spirit world, the rest of the archangels joined Michael and Gabriel. The merging of their mingling lights escapes description in physical language. It is not just that their colors are mostly unknown on earth but also that the colors carry a low humming harmonic. It is more than a sound; the harmonic is alive, energized and energizing; as I waded through the throng of archangels, I experienced a full body, soul-bending, mind-blowing warmth. In my movement among them, the source of all knowledge lived at my fingertips, and at least for the time I was embraced by the angelic group, I had shed the physical world completely. The archangels offered guidance as I moved with and through them: *you must mark your time here.* But I held back a bit longer to enjoy the infinity of being surrounded by the archangels' compassion and love.

When I finally spoke, my voice was soft, distant, unconnected to my everyday world on the earth plane. "I've known them all a long time," I told Douglas. "They're comfortable. They're welcoming me home," I added. "Not home to a physical planet," I clarified; "home . . . *real* home," I said referring to the spirit plane.

The few lines I had spoken had come slowly—*very* slowly—as I continued to opt for the experience, not the narration of it. As someone who has always seen the world as a writer, someone who in general wanted to *describe* a scene more than *experience* it, I was clearly conscious of and somewhat amused about my reticence to report. As I lived the spontaneous, time-drawn encounters on the other side, my earth ego was never far away, however, and the archangels counted on it to kick-start my narration.

You'll have nothing to write about, they teased me.

"I'm not a stranger here," I said in response to the archangels' prodding; "it started on the steps," I added, happy tears filling my eyes. "Michael showed up with Gabriel. Gabriel is on my left. Michael feels on my right, but also he feels everywhere," I tried to explain. "And he joked that he brought a friend."

As I began to tell the story of the ascent to the sacred space, something that had already happened, I was given the opportunity to relive the scene as an onlooker so that my narrative would be strong. Although I was re-experiencing the scene, I continued to progress through the archangel's welcome in the spirit world and, at the same time, begin and end communications with a variety of spirit beings. My mind was also active—another layer to the simultaneous interactions—as it contemplated and tried to characterize all the multi-layered interactions happening all at once. Past, present, and future were fluid, flowing. They were not constrained by any boundaries; in fact, no boundaries existed. Because my storytelling was constrained by time, it took some time to find a rhythm in all the timelessness.

"But Gabriel's more fun," I told Douglas. "He bends his light," I tried to explain. "Michael's a soldier, but Gabriel's the artist," I laughed.

As I told the story to Douglas, Michael made me laugh; he had reacted to the comparison I had made between him and Gabriel by *rolling* his eyes. As he and all in the spirit world were featureless, I *felt* the rolling of his eyes; I did not actually see it.

"On the steps I asked him, something stupid," I admitted, referring to Gabriel. "I asked him why I can't lose weight, and Gabriel said it took a big vessel to hold a big soul. *That* was not the answer I wanted to hear," I laughed out loud.

"Yeah. I bet," Douglas laughed along.

"But it kind of put it in perspective, too," I added as an afterthought. "When I opened the door, they were all there," I said referring to the spirit world. "All of the archangels. And I feel each of their lights," I said. "The smoky one is funny, really funny."

"Did you figure out who that one is?" Douglas asked, referring to my last session in which the smoky one emerged.

"I hear Rag-el, but I . . .."

"Raguel?"

"Maybe."

"Mm-hmm."

"I don't know him," I admitted. "Ahh . . . the lilac is here. The lilac crystal is here," I said, referring to a simultaneous experience outside of the archangel one. "I want to try and explain that," I said meaning the lilac crystal; "but I don't want to forget to tell you about the archangels," I said as a way to goad Douglas on to reminding me if I did. "But first I want to explain the crystal."

"Okay," Douglas agreed.

"If you put a match to silk," I struggled to explain, "the fabric just . . . not tears; it opens. The flame will create a little hole, and the heat of that hole will spread. And that's what the crystal is. As they come—and they're always here," I said referring to The Twelve. "As they come in a," I hesitated searching for the right word. "*Formation* is the word I hear. As they come in a formation, it tears apart the fabric, and then they just wait until I'm fully here."

As a spiritual being experiencing a physical existence, it takes time to adjust to the lack of boundaries in spiritual space. This is because in the physical world, existence is so dense—really dense; in fact, the soul is compressed into a small, thick, constrictive container: a body. Squeezing a soul—even a small fragment of a larger soul—into a human body feels like what we might imagine a genie trapped in a bottle might feel like. Cramped. Claustrophobic. Contained. When the genie is released from such captivity, there is a tsunami of relief. Freedom! Liberation!

In a similar way, when a soul reaches the spirit world, it explodes out into the no-thing-ness of the non-material world and immediately confronts the removal of all physical restrictions, including time. It is a little like the moment when a rollercoaster crests its highest peak and begins the freefall to the valley below; the chest heaves, and breath is momentarily suspended, the head thrusts forward, limbs flutter out of control, and a feeling of weightlessness takes over for just a fraction of a second. Newly released from its physical captivity in a body, the soul similarly flails and pitches and feels disoriented in the simultaneity of it all.

In this particular emergence to the spirit realm, the archangels helped me by weighting my soul with their collective radiance. In effect, they mitigated the effects of my entrance into no-thing-ness from the physical realm of *all*-thing-ness. The more I visit, moreover, the easier and quicker it is for me to remember the feeling, and the more understanding I have of the necessary steps to integrate into the spirit plane from the denseness of the earth.

"The archangels remind me of a basketball team," I laughed, returning to my initial narrative. "They're all around, and they really are teammates. And they know each other so well," I said. "They're not always separate," I added. "They're a powerful, powerful force, but they can split themselves, and that is how we know individual parts of them."

As I discussed the archangels with Douglas, I was given a living history of the archangel realm. They are one part of Source—the everything and the no-thing that cannot be contained. While the archangel's natural state is to be united with Source and with each other, they are given the opportunity to split into component parts for particular needs. When they interact with us on our invitation, we feel their individual vibrations and assign them attributes, some physical, some emotional. While it is not truly the way it is, the archangels allow physical beings to see and experience them in ways that are most comforting to them. So if one person feels a male personality for a particular archangel, the archangel complies by radiating a more male persona; however, if another individual views the same archangel as feminine, the archangel will radiate a more female persona.

"Haniel sticks out because she's short," I laughed as I looked directly at the pink-lit archangel. "She's wide. She reminds me of like a kind of doughty British woman. She's still very regal; it's just that her energy is so down-to-earth which sounds crazy," I said recognizing that there is nothing *earthy* about an archangel. Yet, I understood the expression of her essence as clearly connected to the earth in some way.

"But she's down-to-earth, and she says she spends a lot of time here," I reported as the archangel okayed my description.

"Mm-hmm," Douglas agreed.

"She's the color of the aurora borealis. The pink. The pink that shifts into lilac. The pink," I described in awe at the light spectacle that was Haniel.

Light on the other side is more than visual. It contains sound, a music of some sort, and emotions, memories. Each individual soul experiences the light of the archangels slightly differently. The light of the archangels holds our past encounters with them. All of them. Not just from our current lifetime or one lifetime, but from *all* our lifetimes, and this amalgamation of experiences gives the individual soul a chance to learn why they are and where they have been. It happens effortlessly just by standing in the radiance of the archangels.

"I know the light beings are here. The army. But I'm closed in by the archangels' light, and I can't see them. I can only feel their touches," I noted. "Their light," I said, referring to the archangels, "this will seem weird, but it's like I'm taking a shower in their light. It's just everywhere. All over me. I have the sense of Leonardo da Vinci's *five-pointed man*. I forget what he's called. But like Leonard da Vinci sketched, I'm five-pointed, and the light is coming in and coming out all at the same time," I explained to Douglas by physically spreading my arms out and away from my body. "It's meant to cleanse me."

Vitruvian Man was a pen and ink sketch by Leonard da Vinci; the man stands—arms and legs outspread—in a circle which, in turn, is not completely enclosed in a square. With the help of the drawing, the master attempted to find man's proportion in relation to the earth, and in so doing, focused on finding the universal design at the heart of all creation. Leonardo wrote: "by the ancients man has been called the world in miniature." The goal was to understand the spiritual workings of the universe using one part artistic creation and one

89

part mathematical treatise. As I stood bathed in the archangels' light—arms and legs outspread, as in Leonardo's great masterpiece—my soul-ness was being restored. I was given the chance to remember all my past lives and my complete soul life. Everything I was and am and will be was conveyed to me in the long moments in the archangels' presence.

"The hard part is done," I said cryptically. "I don't know what that means," I added.

Intuitively I expected the declaration meant that I had found my path and that the centuries—millennia, really—of not being able to speak my truth had come to or maybe was coming to an end. It didn't matter which; when I was supposed to know, I would know.

"Now they split open around me," I tell Douglas referring to the archangels. "I look like I have wings now. Like a butterfly," I said while I physically spread my arms to illustrate my words. "Their light," I continued, "is really hot and really cold all at the same time, but it feels amazing. This is some kind of ceremony," I explained; "The colors are beautiful. They're standing so close together," meaning that the six on each side seemed bound to each other, no light intruding in or between their radiance. "Again, like half and half," I said, physically motioning to each side of me. And then, "Michael's behind me."

As I narrated the spectacle of the archangels for Douglas, they split from their formation around me and moved to either side of me. Each side of six moved out in a semicircle. Michael's light moved behind the group and enveloped it completely. Each light maintained its own individual vibration even as it changed and morphed as it merged and separated from and merged again with the light of the others. Light radiated in a multi-color, many-toned, multi-dimensional display of magnificence. It was not stationary; instead, it was moving, alive. There was a sense of eternity, of awe-some-ness, of permanence.

"But they're standing so close together, it crackles," I said about the archangels' light. "Their colors are so different. I can hear it; I can hear the crackle of their lights touching. Like a current. Like a buzzing. An electrical current. But more alive than that," I tried to explain. "I can see it too."

For a moment, my focus shifted from the majesty of the archangels. I did not need to look at them directly to continue to see and experience them; instead, I had begun to learn the rudimentary spirit skill of noting and focusing on concurrent events. To describe them, however, I needed to replace the simultaneity with the constraints of human time, and that made my narrative shift back and forth between events.

"My whole earth family is here," I whispered. "But some of them are . . . they're not all in the same soul group."

As I began greeting my family members in spirit, The Twelve appeared.

"And The Twelve are here. They've presented," I announced. "I feel like I'm in the center of a phoenix and, then, across the front are The Twelve," I said to Douglas. "Hope? Did you guess hope," I asked him referring to a conversation we had about the names of each of The Twelve. "Did you guess hope as one of The Twelve?"

"I think I did," Douglas responded.

"Hope," I said again. "It's different today. It's like a show. Like a light show, but it's not with lights, it's with like a *fire* of colors. I mean it's light, but it crackles, and it moves, and it's living," I said, and a long time ensued before I spoke again. "For the first time, I see it," I finally said, my voice noting my awe. "It's been there all the time."

More than a minute of silence later, Douglas asked, "What do you see?"

"I don't have words," I whispered reverently. "*God* isn't big enough for it," I said referring to the constraints of the human word. "It's Source," I finally announced.

I stood in front of an eternity of authority and light, a power grid so mighty and so unimaginable that my thoughts ceased. I stood staring into it, the brightness so bright that it darkened at the center. It radiated light out all around its edges, and I had the sense of not only observing but also being one with it.

"I'm part and not part at the same time," I reluctantly began my narrative for Douglas. "And I carry it everywhere. We all do," I said. "There're souls of the Astrals," I revealed. "They want me to see," I told Douglas.

"Who's *they*?" Douglas asked for clarification.

The Twelve want me to see I have the wrong idea about Astrals. They are perfect," I explained to Douglas. "Their souls like my soul, like your soul comes from Source. The Twelve are trying to shift my attention, but I can't. I can't turn away," I said, telling him of the struggle not to lose myself in Source. "They are the same," I explained meaning the Astrals. "We are the same, and when we return, we recognize each other," I said, referring to our collective soul life. "And laugh," I giggled. "We play the part of adversaries," I said as Jasmine began to overtake me. "We are not."

There is a point in each hypnotic session when I feel the emergence of The Twelve or, at least, one of The Twelve taking over my physical body. As I stood unwilling to separate myself from Source, I felt The Twelve moving my soul from it to them. They allowed my ego to remain engaged in the spectacle of Source while Jasmine's soul—my soul—reemerged with the part that resides in my physical body. This process is not manipulative or scary or uncomfortable in any way. In fact, it is my natural state; this uniting with my full soul is a profound and, to be honest, satisfactory pull; it mirrors the work of a magnet as it picks up iron fillings, except that there is no difference between the pulled and the attractor in the spirit realm. We— Jasmine and I—are simply pieces of a whole.

"It's a part we play," I continued talking about the Astrals. "And they're pure and clear and radiant. In the physical form, their story traps them. They deserve our compassion. I wanted to say *pity*," I said, my ego reemerging; "but they stopped me from *pity*. Compassion," I said and, then, Jasmine took over the narrative,

A Message from The Twelve: Love Breaks the Stranglehold of the Story

"And their story effects all of our institutions on earth even religion," Jasmine began to speak through me about the Astrals. "They tried to clear that before. That was Jesus's mission. He was a man, the same. Just a being. The same," she said connecting his physical form to mine, to Douglas's, to every physical being's. "He had a mission, and his mission worked for a little while," she explained.

On the spiritual plane, I was given the opportunity to review the life of Jesus from Jesus's point of view. I smelled the dryness of the air, a grittiness of sand and dirt and olive tree. I felt the tiny split in his lip from the lack of humidity, and the feel of the arid ground under his feet, the skin on his heals cracking, dry, pained. I heard his thoughts and felt a combination of spiritual knowing and human fear; I heard the tone and timbre of his voice—gentle, but strong, lion and lamb combined—as he replied to those around him. I lived the mystical history that I had been taught to revere as a child.

"And you know what?"

"Hm?"

"His soul," Jasmine said referring to Jesus, "looks the same as the Astrals'. This is what we need to know. If we fulfill our role as adversary to the Astrals, the message does not come clear. They are us. We are all manifestation of Source, she explained. "We understood the last time," she said referring to a past hypnotic session, "that they have manipulated our population. And they have. That's their story. But the story we're stuck in, accepts it," she said. After a long silence, Jasmine continued, "In their story, they found what they thought was a weakness in the human story. They felt the joy emanation was weak."

"I'm sorry. What was weak again?" Douglas asked.

"The emanation of joy from humans."

"Mm."

"That's our mission, but the Astrals looked for what they thought was weak. That's their story," she explained. "And they found the joy vibration: the need to link in joy to each other. That's something they could manipulate, and they did. They used their own gift against us, but *our* story didn't allow us to see it," Jasmine explained. "We accepted it. We accepted it as *this is the way it is, this is the way it's always been.* And we forget that it's *just* a story we've built for ourselves."

I began to see the role of humanity in our own manipulation.

We're not victims? I asked.

Yes, but not in the way you've imagined it, Jasmine replied even as she spoke through me to Douglas. *You are the victims of your own story, and in taking the role of manipulators, the Astrals are the victims of their story,* she explained.

In the previous hypnotic sessions, I had considered the Astrals the bad guys; humanity, in my understanding, became the hapless victims of Astral cruelty. But it was much more complicated. We—humanity—had a part to play on the path to destruction we now find ourselves. The Astrals could not have done it without us; it was up to humanity and those who have traveled from outside star systems to incarnate as humans to move the current course away from destruction.

You must accept your part, Jasmine warned.

Otherwise, she helped me understand, we simply replicated the Astral's story in a new way. We might give up linking in hate against our own—human *others*, in other words, but we would simply choose instead to band together in hate against the Astral *other*. Transferring hate from an in-group to an out-group, in other words, continued the story of the Astrals; we would still link in *hate*, not joy. Instead, it was on us to stop the cycle of hate. I reflected on the gift of meeting Astral souls as I stood in awe of Source; The Twelve had concocted a brilliant strategy to drive home a point. As I met my Astral soul-mate and recognized our sameness, I understood the message I was intended to share. We do not fight against the Astrals; instead, we commit to breaking through our own story to find our Source vibration. On the earth plane, our natural vibration is joy.

"The Astrals found the ingredient. The ingredient is hate," Jasmine spoke through me. "They mixed their hate into our cocktail of joy that comes from linking. And we confused the joy of linking with the extra ingredient. It's not hatred that brings us joy. It's not being better than the *other* that brings us joy. It's uniting. All of us together to sing our song of joy for the universe," she explained. "The Astrals' mission was to tend this," she said.

"I'm sorry. The Astrals' mission was to?" Douglas trailed off.

"Tend," Jasmine answered. Her voice sounded far-away, slow, deliberate.

"Hm."

"Like gardeners. They were more advanced—much more advanced—than the human population," she explained. After a long, thoughtful silence, Jasmine continued, "in the beginning, they wanted to cultivate the joy for themselves to the exclusion of others. That was the start," she explained. "So misguided," she smiled. "It's vibration. The vibration fills the world and moves out through the universes. You can't contain it," she laughed as she continued the history of the Astrals. "For as advanced as they were, they couldn't understand that. They *still* don't understand it," she concluded. "It's infinite. You don't have to contain it, so you get more," Jasmine chuckled. "It's infinite. Joy is infinite," she repeated.

As Jasmine spoke through me to Douglas, she was able to look out from my eyes to the sensual earth. While it is dense for such an enlightened soul, she reveled in her ability to *experience* sensations. It did not matter that my eyes were closed in deep meditation or that my physical body was constrained by four walls. Jasmine was, as she could be in the spirit realm, many places completing many tasks at the same time. Even on earth. While she could visit whenever she wanted, the physical impressions of the earth realm were only *really* available to her through a physical body. Today it was mine.

"As they began to cultivate joy, the Astrals had to create the *other*. They did this because earth beings are fundamentally—because of their joy—fundamentally naïve in earth terms. Or too trusting in earth terms," she explained. "But in the spirit realm, it is not naïve or trusting, it just is. Joy is joy," she pronounced.

When Jasmine spoke of joy, she exuded it. Her vibration—her role in the universes—was to emanate and direct the joy vibration, and she was most in tune with her soul's purpose when she was doing it. During the times when she spoke of it, therefore, her vibration increased as if the mere mention of it gave her the incentive to harness and magnify the joy throughout the universes. Everything and everyone in its pathway was bathed in the light of joy.

"So when the Astrals began to cultivate the joy," Jasmine continued, "the light in the human population would go out. Like using a snuff to put out a candle," she explained. "A boy on a summer's night catches a firefly in a jar to harness the light for himself, and the firefly dies, and the light dies with it. And this was the problem the Astrals experienced with their plan to harness joy from humanity."

Jasmine's metaphor of the boy, the jar, and the firefly's death brought about a reliving of a childhood memory. One of my earliest recollections came when I was very young, maybe three or four years old. My father's uncle—Eddie—had appeared at our doorstep one afternoon to introduce himself. My father had never before met his Uncle Eddie; in fact, he did not know his father had brothers. Uncle Eddie and his brother—my father's father—had been fighting for most of their lives. One day, Uncle Eddie had the revelation that he couldn't remember why they fought, so he sought out his brother's children as a way of *almost* repairing the breach between brothers.

On one of the first nights of Uncle Eddie's first visit, he took me into the front yard of my childhood home. The crickets chirped in the cool summer night of a mountain July. There was only a sliver of moon, so in spite of the multitudinous stars that shone on the black dome of the sky of my childhood memory, it was quite dark. Except for the tip of Uncle Eddie's lit pipe. The smell of that pipe has imprinted itself in my little girl's memory; it was glorious, almost musical in its sonorous smell.

"Look at the firefly," Uncle Eddie said, holding his hand out to mine.

He gently, gingerly placed the firefly in my hand, and I remember the joy of his careful, quiet touch and the light of the living being on the meat of my pudgy little hand.

"Be careful with 'em," Uncle Eddie warned. "Their light is God's," he said, as he leaned back into his pipe. "If you hold onto 'em," he added, "they'll die."

I fluttered my hand to release the firefly. Even as a young child, I did not want such an awesome responsibility.

"Oh, you can enjoy the light," Uncle Eddie said. "Just be responsible with it."

That scene with Uncle Eddie resonated so strongly with my heart; for most of my life, it showed up at strange times, and its power overwhelmed me. "Just be responsible with it," I heard in relation to the light. I now understood the childhood memory as a life lesson I needed to learn. In her words, Jasmine rekindled the story to help me remember.

"Because humans are fundamentally joy," Jasmine continued, "the Astrals had to steel themselves for what they were doing. They felt it. They felt each snuffing out of the light," she explained. "Each one a prick of pain. That's written into their DNA now," she said sadly.

"What's in their DNA?" Douglas interrupted Jasmine.

"The memory of all the pain they've caused. They have to *push* it away. So, as they wrote their story; earth beings became *unsophisticated*, let's say. Unsophisticated in the eyes of the Astrals, and they experimented on not a *worthy* population, but on an *unsophisticated, unworthy* population. But only in their minds," she clarified for Douglas. "And they found hate. And hate worked. And because earth beings are naïve and trusting," she continued her explanation, "they accepted the cloak and wore it proudly. And they began to associate joy with the division that hate created. *My team, not your team*," Jasmine said. "And they began to write *their* story to include hate and division," she said referring to humanity. "Hate has many forms. Many forms," she repeated. "And over millennia, Astrals have told their story, and earth beings have written it into theirs, and they've become entangled," she said. "This message is for earth beings," she disclosed. "There are others on missions to help rewrite the story of the Astrals." And, then, after a short silence, she added, "they will bring each other's downfall."

"Who's they?" Douglas asked.

"The Astrals and the humans. And yet their stories are woven together," Jasmine laughed; "they don't realize that they have more in common than not. And that is the first part of the message," she announced. "You may ask," Jasmine told Douglas after a long silence.

"I'm presuming we're talking about the Ananaki?" Douglas asked about a mythical extraterrestrial group.

"They are known *here* by that name. There is not just one."

"Mm-hmm," Douglas agreed.

"While your soul base comes from the orange star; hers comes from the Pleiades. Yet you are close. Too close to differentiate between the people," Jasmine said in answer to Douglas's question and referring to Douglas and me respectively. "And so it is with the Astrals. There are several. Do not oppose them now. That is the lesson the Stellars must learn."

"Can you say more about that, so I can conceptualize what you're saying?" Douglas asked.

"Yes," Jasmine replied. "There are many wonderful, good things about Stellars. They are close to Source. They understand," she added, "but this is their hubris. They use it—not intentionally—to create the *other*. So, they learned the Astrals' story as well," she said definitively. "There are groups that are recognizing, understanding this, and dropping it. They are embracing the Astrals, and this is having an effect," Jasmine said.

"Who is embracing the Astrals?" Douglas asked.

"There are some Stellar groups and some *parts* of Stellar groups that have recognized an adversarial relationship is not effective. They are breaking free of the Astrals' story."

"By the embracing?" Douglas asked.

"Yes," Jasmine replied. "By embracing the *soul* of the Astrals, not the *actions* of the Astrals. The actions are part of their story," she explained. "Imagine you found a rock and inside the rock, you can see just the very tip of a diamond. You know it's in there," she said, "but you have to be careful as you free the diamond," she cautioned. "Some Stellar groups have taken that as a metaphor for the Astrals," she confirmed. "They are exposing the light, not hurting their physical existence."

"So, you are talking about the Stellars who are embracing the Astrals?" Douglas asked.

"Yes," Jasmine replied. "Not all of your group does."

"What group are we referring to now?"

"Your soul group from the orange star. Some do," she continued. "But it's still debated, and this is nothing to feel embarrassed about. It's an open, intellectual, and honest debate, and they will find their way," Jasmine assured Douglas. "They are living their missions."

"Tell me why," Douglas began. "Maybe giving me this will help me understand because I'm hearing your words, but I'm not integrating it. When I use the word *cabal*...," he trailed off.

"Ah-hah."

"What about the energy of that word is problematic?"

"Yes," Jasmine began her answer. "Cabal understands the *other*. It requires the *other*, a being who does what I would *not* do. Not a being who is like me. Your world is mission driven. Your soul is mission driven. Your mission is to promote peace, to protect. Very worthy," she concluded. "And you recognize the group of Astrals that bring havoc to the peace you desire."

"Okay," Douglas kind of agreed.

"And you've taken them as adversaries, yet you know that they are you, and you are they. We are all part of Source. They—we—emanate from and reflect back to Source," Jasmine said. Cabal suggests something . . . maybe *nefarious*, we'll say."

"Mm-hmm," Douglas agreed.

"Something that's not part of who you are, but you are part of the cabal you set up for Astrals because *they* are you, and you are *they*. So if you create cabals for them, you've created cabals for you. Do you see?"

"Hm. Not really," Douglas confessed.

"It's a reflection."

"Yes."

"You're the same."

"There are belief systems I hold that interfere with me being able to integrate this at this moment," Douglas admitted.

"Yes, and that's okay."

"Good thing," Douglas chuckled.

"Yes," Jasmine answered seriously. "Yes, it takes time."

"Yeah. I'm just trying to wrap my head around enough of it so that I can work with it."

"When the sun hits the diamond in the rock," Jasmine returned to an earlier metaphor, "the diamond will heat up. The rock will fissure. The diamond will emerge unscathed. Love is *that* type of light."

"Love?"

"Love," Jasmine assured him.

"Yeah."

"It creates the situation . . . the instance . . . to let the light in . . . to let the light of the Astral emerge," Jasmine continued.

"Mm-hmm."

"It is not easy. It is not easy," she reiterated. "But you asked before about the children of a union between Astral and human," Jasmine reminded Douglas of a question from a prior session.

"Mm-hmm."

"And how the touch of a child's tiny hand can change the heart and the *story* of an Astral. If a child's hand can make that happen, what can a great light warrior's love do?" she asked.

"You better hurry up and find some," Douglas joked.

"Find some?"

"Great warriors."

"Oh!" she exclaimed. "So, you do not know yourself?" Jasmine joked with Douglas.

"Well, I'm struggling with that," Douglas laughed.

"Peace. You can be a warrior and be peaceful. In fact, you are a better warrior if you are peaceful," she explained.

"Mm-hmm."

"The Arcturians are *known* for peace. This is their mission. It's their vibration, but they are *great* warriors."

"Yeah," Douglas began; "I find that whole *paradox*—it's the only word I can come up with—is that they talk about peace, and they also talk about having the most powerful weapon in the universe. *As far as they know*, they always qualify. But it's an interesting juxtaposition."

"There is strength in peace as there is strength in joy on the earth level. Great strength, but it must be harnessed and focused in the right way. They are willing to go to battle if needed. The Arcturians."

"Mm-hmm."

"But that is *after* every attempt at peace because they know when they go to battle, they disrupt the peace vibration. Not just for them. Not just for the *other*. But for the whole universe. And since their mission is to emanate peace, the vibration throughout all universes, going to battle is the last step."

"Mm-hmm."

"It is a step of dimensions; it is not a step that happens in the spirit world," Jasmine said. "It's the denseness and the physical nature of your beings. You will get to a point where you will no longer battle; it will not be the last step. The last step will be peace."

"It's interesting," Douglas interrupted silence; "because what you say resonates well within me which is very interesting because my mind cannot grasp it."

"Your mind is human now," she soothed.

"It would seem so."

"Yes."

"You're saying there's a release because it resonates in a way that seems *oh good*. I didn't even know there was an *oh good*," Douglas admitted.

"It's very good. In fact," Jasmine continued, "it is you soul mission. It is your soul level. The soul of an Arcturian or the soul of a Stellar or the soul of an Astral or the soul of a Pleiadean; there is no difference except for the mission," she explained. "She," Jasmine said referring specifically to me, "feels a sense of homesickness, of longing for her other world, but all she's looking for is the emanation where she fits in. Your emanation is peace," Jasmine said to Douglas. "Your vibration is peace, and you're conflicted at the human level, because their emanation is joy. So, your brain has a hard time taking both together, and when we add the manipulation from the Astrals, you are conflicted, but it's just physical."

"Hm. I like your putting *just*," Douglas joked.

"Yes. Yes," Jasmine responded in kind. "This time that you spend in this form is but nothing. It seems like something here on the earth, but it's like your summer vacation to the ocean. It's finished," she said wiping the palms of my hands together to illustrate the finality. "You get there on Sunday and feel an eternity of time in front of you for one week, and yet too quickly you're packing your car to go home," she explained. "That is the conflict of the earth timing. Arcturians don't feel time," she instructed. "Did that help?" Jasmine asked after a long pause.

"Some," Douglas answered. "I'm trying to build out what I know of what you're sharing and trying to integrate that and doing poorly."

"No. No," Jasmine countered; "you will always be conflicted; this you must accept. Your soul base radiates peace; this planet radiates joy. Even though both are good vibrations, they're not your vibrations. The joy is not yours," she explained. "And Arcturians don't recognize time; humans do. Another conflict," she added.

"So, I'm sorry; I'm trying to figure it out. What vibrations do Arcturians hold and emanate?" Douglas asked.

"Peace."

"Peace."

"It is their mission. That's why they are the guardians," she said. Then, after a silence in which she waited for Douglas's confirmation, she explained it another way, "Arcturians are evolved, and they emanate peace, and they feel when they go to battle that it is their last resort. And they make this calculation wisely," Jasmine allowed, "but in making the calculation, they've forgotten that peace is more powerful. They fall into a trap. The goal is to emanate more peace so that peace remains," she affirmed, and after a brief silence, she added, "but that will come."

"How does this all fit in with beings from the Angelic realm?" Douglas asked.

"The Angelic realm is everywhere," Jasmine began her answer. "They're infinite. Their light and their being are able to be parsed everywhere at the same time, but the Angelic realm is forbidden to interfere by Source unless *asked*."

In this explanation, Jasmine was affirming the gift of free will that all physical and spiritual beings receive from Source. While the angelic realm have the capacity, duty, and desire to support all beings, they must receive permission before interfering in their capacity for free will. Once asked—once given permission—the angelic realm will step in with aid and comfort.

"Their vibrations match," she continued to answer Douglas's question, "but they can shift when needed. Michael emanates strength through compassion, but when he needs to," she explained, "he can emanate another vibration. Gabriel emanates clarity, but when he needs it, he can emanate the vibration of strength through compassion. These help the physical beings remember. They help remember their mission. The Angelic realm are the foot soldiers of Source, and they never resort to battle. Their strength is in their vibrations."

"And their vibration is of love?" Douglas asked.

"Love and every part of love. The spectrum of love. Love comes in many, many forms."

"Mm-hmm."

"And the archangels can radiate the whole spectrum of love."

"Can you help me understand why in the future . . . in the near future . . . on earth, there is going to be a battle?"

"So again, constrained by earth's thinking, it appears to be a battle. Yes? But it's more metaphoric," she explained. "It's a battle between ideologies: do earth beings keep their story and refuse to give up that story and, therefore, believe that hate is the link that makes them happy?" she asked in illustration. "And hatred, like love, has a spectrum," she explained. "So division might be a better way to explain it. Division. Have they accepted division so clearly that they can't break free of their story," she said referring to humanity. "And will the Astrals still protect their own story so that they create the conditions for the end? "And the answer is yes on the path we're on," she said. "And that is why these vibrations have increased."

Vibrations are like living electrical currents. There is nothing inert, nothing that is not alive on the spirit realm; vibrations, then, are no different from everything else. Their currents pass like shockwaves throughout the physical realm, disrupting and disturbing the natural order. Like defibrillation, which is meant to save the physical body, the shock will sometimes instead create havoc and, on some occasions, death. Yet, humanity continues to use defibrillation because, on the whole, its shock to a human system has a positive effect. So, while the vibrations the archangels transmit are intended to radiate the help that may ultimately save the earth and humanity from final destruction, using them has unintended, sometimes dire consequences in the physical realm.

"But vibrations come at a cost on the physical plane," Jasmine explained. "If we increase the intensity, we see a physical recognition: earthquakes and flooding, volcanoes, all kinds of severe weather. The earth—the physical earth—will respond to the increase of vibration. Imagine in a pool—a small pool of water," she instructed. "If you put a current—a strong current—into the water, the water will ripple and move. And this is what you must imagine is coming from an increase in vibration," she explained. "The chaos that comes on the earth is not a symptom of the hatred, but a manifestation of the vibration. It is unfortunate."

Jasmine stopped to consider the arsenal that humanity has built in its rush to hatred. *They believe such things protect,* she said. I waited for her to explain, but she left the thought as is. It was more powerful unfinished.

"A single act on the earth level can destroy the earth," she said. "You have the capability to destroy the earth, but not the sophistication to understand that it's *final.* So in balance, using the vibrations even if it causes physical disruption, is . . . I grasped for the word . . . not *better,* not *regrettable,* but perhaps the only way."

"I'm sorry; what is the only way?" Douglas asked.

"The increase in vibration."

"Where does the increase in vibration come from?"

"Archangels. This is the answer to your question."

"Mm-hmm."

There is a long silence as Jasmine speaks to me. I have seen the chaos and destruction of which she speaks, and it terrifies me. It is personal. I have seen the faces of those I know and love anguished, desperate, alone.

It may not come to pass, she says as she wraps her spiritual body around me. *It is time to return*, she whispers into my hair.

No, I cry.

I have adjusted to the weightlessness, the timelessness, the no-thing-ness. I feel unencumbered, joyous, and I do not want to return to the density, pain, and pressure of the physical plane.

"I'm afraid we might have shown her too much now," Jasmine admitted to Douglas. "I'll have Michael bring her back."

"Okay. Thank you for chatting today."

"You are a warrior," Jasmine concluded, speaking directly to Douglas. "And while I know you will doubt yourself, I would like to tell you not to."

"I appreciate the thought."

In the swirl and churn of dis-uniting from Jasmine's soul—from my soul, I had the sensation of being sucked through the end of a straw and dumped into the waiting light of Archangel Michael. *No*, I whined, and he drew me closer into his radiance. Flowing, sparkling white light rained down on me, and I was once again reminded of Leonardo's *Vitruvian Man* as I spread my limbs to bathe in Michael's eternity.

Once I submitted to the light, my fear vanished, and Michael led me to the door away from the spiritual realm and, once through its threshold, into the physical realm. While it only took a few moments in the physical as Douglas awaited my return, I stood in the spiritual shower of Michael's brilliance for hours, maybe days. The spirit touches of light beings and my earth family, of people I knew, of those I didn't, and of the immediate embrace of The Twelve found me, ghost-like, gentle, soft, and I allowed them to remind me who I was and where I've been and what I'm destined to do. When they pulled back from me, I nodded to Michael, and together, we walked through the door to the physical realm.

When I opened my eyes, I was groggy, not fully consciousness, but aware of the heaviness that had returned to my limbs.

"Welcome back," Douglas said.

ACT IV

The Cosmos is Within Us

13 June 2019

*Our birth is but a sleep and a forgetting; the
soul that rises with us, our life's star, hath had
elsewhere its setting, and cometh from afar.*
Williams Wordsworth

Negativity Finds Me . . .
For a Little While At Least

But that shadow has been serving you!
What hurts you, blesses you.
Darkness is your candle.
Your boundaries are your quest.
~Jalal al Din Muhammad Rumi

As I prepared for the next hypnotic session with Douglas, I found myself juggling and, then, obsessing about the sudden negative changes in my life. I had just found out my husband would spend another year in Dubai, finishing out his teaching contract and living much too far away. There were mounting bills and a bank account that could not keep up—a $5000 IRS bill and new brakes, for example. I also pulled a muscle performing a menial task that messed-up my back, and what's more, I had been having dreams of dread and threats that kept me up at night. On top of it all, I was moving to a new apartment. Each day I would pack the car, drive to the new apartment, unload, unpack, drive back, pack up again, and load the car once more. Rinse and repeat. Day after day. Early one sunny morning in the shade of the still snow-capped Rockies, I packed the car and set out to the new apartment. As I looked to the mountains, I felt the beauty of nature and forgot all about the rest. I recognized my eternity in the landscape.

"Thank you. Thank you. Thank you," I whispered over and over again.

But the *ding!* of a new text message drew my thoughts back inside the car and away from the mountains. I lifted the phone to see a name in the header. **Maybe: Jasmine**, it said, and the part of the text I could see without opening said *You may reply to this message.*

"Weird," I gasped, but because I was driving, the rest of the text remained unread. "You could help," I replied out loud to the message. "You could provide the means to make this easier," I said.

For the weeks between the second and fourth sessions, I had the sense that the negative piling on was a result of the message I was transmitting. I recalled the long list of rules I consented to in front of The Twelve during my first session. While I had concentrated on the warnings about sickness and the potential loss of years from my life, I had almost completely ignored the one about negativity. Actually, it didn't seem that bad to me. In comparison to breast cancer or death, I mean. I would attract negativity, The Twelve cautioned me, because there would be some entities who would want to stop me from delivering the message.

"Now you reply to me," I said out loud to Jasmine. "Why can't you make this easier on me? At least financially."

You didn't ask, I heard in reply.

And, just like that, I felt Jasmine moving into the crowded space of my overpacked car. I knew it was her—or I knew it was me, I guess—because I recognized the feeling I had in the hypnotic sessions. When Jasmine had come before, she crowded out everything else—thoughts, feelings, even air. There was a certain heaviness that surrounded me, and my chest heaved in an attempt to get enough oxygen into my lungs. The feeling was unmistakable on that blue-skied morning when the white clouds seemed to reach down just enough from the Heavens to touch the white peaks of the mountains.

"I didn't know I had to ask," I answered. "Why is this happening?"

The Astrals are aware, she warned, and I felt the omnipresence of Archangel Michael as proof of her words. *They felt the vibration.*

"And?" I asked. Although I was skeptical about the conversation I was having, I was still interested in the answer. Just in case.

And they are working to get you to stop.

"Great," I said sarcastically.

And it will last until we know you will continue, she said.

"How long?" I asked.

A few weeks more, she admitted.

"And you can't help me?"

We already are, she said. *We are laying the groundwork, but you must continue with the process. They won't stop just because you do,* she told me.

In my gut, I believed that writing up the fourth session would be the turning point, and I counted on it as the week progressed. Until I laid on the floor of the new apartment in pain. I waited, waited, waited for the moment when I would feel the pain in my back subside enough to move. It took a couple of hours. Not long after, I emailed Douglas about rescheduling. I could not sit long enough at the computer to write, and I understood that I could not sit for the next session until I did.

Point: Astrals.

The Fourth Hypnotic Session: Stellars and Astrals and Ships. Oh My!

The session began as usual with a little chit-chat, a check-in, and a count to my sacred space.

"Deep. Deeper. Deepest. You're at the door to your sacred space," Douglas said. "Go ahead and open it, Jackie. Step through, and when you're ready, close it behind you."

After a long silence, I began to narrate, "Everything is really fast. I don't know why. I can't really focus on anything because it's moving so quickly in front of me."

"Does Michael have a suggestion?" Douglas asked after another lengthy silence.

"Back up," I whispered after asking Michael for help. "Back up?" I asked the archangel. "Oh," I said with some clarity, "I'm just supposed to tell you about the steps until it settles for me."

"Okay," Douglas agreed.

"Oh, I know why," I said, referring back to my inability to focus.

When hypnotized, I am fully aware of being in Douglas's office; I am fully aware of what I say. Time and tone are lost, but everything else remains normal. Hearing myself in a hypnotic state is always unsettling, however. While I have some control over the words that come out of my mouth, I feel compelled to speak, compelled to narrate the scene in front of me. At times, there can be an internal struggle when my concern for what others might think about my words becomes more important than what the words are meant to convey. I feel the struggle most profoundly when I am asked to narrate anything that has to do with Star people. In earth terms, *aliens*. When I become aware that I am about to discuss the Stellars or the Astrals or anything that has to do with their home environments in the stars, the struggle becomes an epic battle within me. After a lifetime of accepting the reaction of others when they learn I can see and hear spirit, I am generally okay with spirit. But aliens? Well, that's another issue altogether.

So, when I finally recognized that I stood on the bridge of a Stellar ship, I cringed.

No, I whined.

You must speak, I heard very clearly.

Not aliens, I whined again adding a sense of stomping my foot in protest.

Not aliens, I heard in a mild admonishment. *They are souls having a physical experience. Like you.*

I replied, *not like me.*

My mind and experience fields were filled with TV pseudo-documentaries focused on interstellar intelligent life; I felt the campiness crawl through my craw. I relived my own judgement of the men and women "scholars" who presented what, in their opinions, were facts that led to the inescapable conclusion that we were not alone. *They're just like you*, the spirit world reinforced. They were resolute that I would speak. I knew I would. I knew I must, but I was still reticent about indicting myself as an ancient astronaut expert.

"I'm with," I hesitated, still resisting. "I'm with the Stellars. And I'm not used to, or I can't keep up with the dimension. But I could start," I said and, then, stopped. "It's uncomfortable actually. I can't even tell you what I'm looking at because it's moving," I said clearly disoriented. "Do you remember the old reels with newspapers on?"

"Mm-hmm."

"And you'd press the button and watch it move on the screen?"

"Right."

"But sometimes you would press it too fast and *fsssst*," I explained mimicking the sound of the tape running out and off the reel.

"Mm-hmm. Right."

"That's what it's doing."

Archangel Michael assured me it would change; he assured me I would adjust at least a little. *Be patient*, he advised. I closed my eyes and covered them with the palms of my hands. I needed to stop the movement. I was in migraine territory.

"So, Michael says just start with the steps until it settles for me." I laughed as I recalled the floating staircase, "Something weird happened today on the steps. He came late," I said meaning Archangel Michael. "He came up maybe at nine," I said referring to Douglas' count. "Which is unusual; he usually meets me at the beginning, but I felt like Noah walking up the steps because there were so many animals. It was like a menagerie," I said quickly. "Even a tiger was there, and it was just for fun. It was beautiful. I mean they were spilling onto the steps and off of the steps, and," I suddenly stopped. "Oh, it's settled," I announced and immediately moved off the steps and back to the bridge of the Stellar ship.

"The Stellars did something to settle me," I explained although I wasn't quite sure what they had done. As they explained, I listened. "And here comes the light. Here come The Twelve," I said even as I continued to listen to the Stellars' explanations. "But this time they're coming not through the fabric of," I said and grappled for the right words. "They're not coming through the fabric of the spirit world. They're in physical space," I announced. "This is a big deal. This is a big deal," I reiterated.

"In what way?" Douglas asked.

"The Federation is waiting for them. They knew they were coming," I answered. "And there are hundreds of ships. It doesn't matter that we're in separate ships because we can hear each other," I said and, then, pointed to the right in physical space. "There's mine," I said. "There's mine. There's mine," I said again and again. "Right there."

"That's your ship?" Douglas asked.

"Yeah. My people," I responded. "They're crystals," I said.

Not this, I heard and stopped speaking.

The topic was, I understood immediately, not allowed. At least, for human consumption. To explain what I saw and what I knew would reveal a universal secret that humans were not yet sophisticated enough to accept. Now as I write, I have no memory that would clarify the statement. Even for me. That is the way sometimes.

"I can understand everybody's thoughts," I changed direction.

"I'm sorry," Douglas interrupted. "You can or you can't?"

"I can," I answered. "It's not like in the spirit world where I," I hesitated. "It's not like in the spirit world where it's just natural; it's just remembering how to do it. Here, they've implanted something kind of like what they wear at the UN to understand different languages," I said motioning to just below my right ear.

"Mm-hmm."

"But it's a single language; it's not English," I tried to explain. "You know, somehow I understand it, and that's technology, too. And they—the Stellars—told me that," I said and, then, stopped for a long silence as I listened to the Stellars explain, "it's technology. Advanced."

While I spoke to Douglas about technology, I heard the many languages that merged—an amalgam of many—into one to form a single language. Not mine. Not theirs either. Or anyone's for that matter. The Stellars explained it was a pure language; it was uncorrupted by physical beings. It was language in its purest sense before the interference of the physical realm, and because it was untouched, it was understood at the gut level, at the spiritual level. There was a place in all of us—regardless of origin—that resonated with its purity. We understood it at the soul level, and there was no need for translation. The technology only enhanced our ability to remember.

"I'm on the bridge of the aircraft carrier-like ship."

I stopped to search my memory for the film images of my youth: *The Enterprise* and *The Millennium Falcon,* among them. But the comparison was faulty at its core. Those representations of ships were conceived based on the physical constraints of earth and our novice understanding of technology. There was no analogy I could make, so I decided to simply describe what I saw.

"There are no buttons or anything like that," I began. "It's all sleek. It's all done with thought; it's not manual," I explained, noting the biggest difference between what I had known and what I now saw. "The window curves down," I began my description, "and then it's titanium housing. It's interesting because there are no edges," I noted, but my attention was drawn to the business of the beings on board the ship. The focus of the day's gathering became clearer. "They heard the message. They heard the message last week," I said. An awareness of tension slowly emerged for me. "They didn't like it."

"Mm-hmm," Douglas said in a way that suggested *this is going to be good.*

"And there's fear. The fear is palpable. You can physically see fear," I said. "It's the dimension that allows feelings to be physically ... *physical*'s not the right word," I corrected myself. A long silence ensued as I grappled with a way to describe what I knew. "It's kind of hard for me in this dimension," I explained. "Things aren't as clear for me as they are in the spirit world. I'm disoriented. They had to slow it down for me, but it has this weird effect like if you ever watched the movie *Godzilla*," I laughed. "And the mouths of the characters are moving speaking Japanese, but the English words come out of it."

"Mm-hmm."

"That's how I'm experiencing this. I'm just kind of out of ... I'm a step out of time with everything. It's a delay for me," I explained. "If you can imagine ships—just hundreds of them—in a formation looking in. Into space. And there's no dais or anything like that, but The Twelve are in the middle. Their physical presence is different," I said. "They're more transparent. They're less colorful and less musical," I noted. "It's because it's denser," I explained. They're ascended. They're ascended," I repeated. "The Twelve."

Although I had already intuited that The Twelve were Ascended Masters, to *hear* them acknowledge it was a big deal. The Ascended, I understood, had once had physical incarnations, yet after many spiritual trials and successes, they transformed into higher-level spirit beings. Their transformations brought them very close to Source, very close to the core of everything and no-thing-ness. Although they can, they have chosen *not* to reconnect with Source until all other souls have returned. They are the bodhisattvas. They are the enlightened ones. They are The Twelve.

"And the archangels are here," I continued to describe the scene. "I really like them," I said referring to the archangels.

A mere observer, I simply watched the events transpire. And narrated them for Douglas. I felt the quickness of the Stellars as they prepared to lay out their arguments against the Astrals. I felt their awe at the spirit spectacle in front of them; even though the Stellars were able to transcend the physical boundaries in order to interact with the spirit world, they had not expected The Twelve to appear in physical space. Rather, they prepared to interact with The Twelve in a spiritual forum. It was the first time they had actually *seen* The Twelve, and while I recognized the muted colors and dampened harmonics of The Twelve in physical form, the Stellars only saw a spectacular, multimodal display.

"They want me to tell you what the Arcturians look like," I said sheepishly.

"I've been wondering," Douglas responded.

"But they're really angry, so it's kind of funny. It's visible on them," I said meaning anger. "I don't want to insult them," I said giggling, "they're really tall, but when they're angry, they," I stopped not wanting to offend, but enjoying the display too much not to continue. "When they're angry, they *shrink*," I said. "This was an adaptation for them because they vibrate peace. Just like when we get angry, we redden; it's a marker that we're off our normal vibration."

After a few minutes, I regained my composure because the Arcturians in front of me flashed *the look*. But like a train wreck, I could not stop looking, staring, sniggering. When the Arcturians explained it away as an adaptation—all serious and science-like—it only made me more interested.

It is a good adaptation, one told me.

I agree, I said as I giggled.

I got the distinct feeling the Stellars were rolling their eyes at my childish behavior. Since their eyes were bigger, more oval, and without discernible eyelids and lashes, the eye rolling was only a feeling, not a physical reality.

"I know I'm not supposed to find it funny, but it really is kind of funny. When they get angry, they shrink down. The Arcturians," I explained. "But in general, they're really tall, and they have a spinal cord that's very evident," I said as I air-traced the spinal cord in Douglas's office. "Almost reptilian, the spinal cord. And it comes up to the base of their cranium. Very thin," I explained. "Their necks are longer, and their faces are more angular. I mean . . . they're different, but they're humanoid-looking," I said, trying to connect with the similarities. "Tapered. Their hands are tapered, and I would say, regal. They look regal," I said and added, "except when they get angry." I felt the phantom eye-rolling once again. *Earthling*, I thought I heard them think.

"I don't see anything like hair, but their eyes are deeper set," I said and, then, realized something wasn't right. "But I have to correct myself because it's not that they don't have hair either. I don't know if I can't see it because of the dimension change."

Although there wasn't anything physical I could do to change the way I was experiencing the Stellar dimension, I squinted and shaded my eyes, hoping to make a difference. The movement of time was visible to me; I could actually see time. Like a thin haze of multi-colored striations, the kind that you might find on an old TV with a scrambled signal, this visual layer compounded the difficulty I had concentrating. When I finally forced myself to focus on my surroundings, I noticed another group of Stellars. Not Arcturians. Because the Stellars were so tall and angular, I had not noticed the other group; they stood at least one-half the height of the Arcturians.

"There's another group of Stellars," I reported to Douglas. "They're maybe three or four feet, and they're wider. And although they have arms and legs and a head, they don't have much of a neck, and their skin is *really* thick."

As I began my description of the others on board the Federation transporter, I noticed the feelings of the Arcturians invading my physical space. Their emotions had piqued as The Twelve listened to their complaints.

"The Arcturians are feeling put upon," I announced.

"Because?" Douglas whispered.

"Because they're the peacekeepers, and last week's message took their most persuasive tool from them."

"You mean their advanced weapons?" Douglas asked.

"Yes."

"Yes."

"Yes, they're like children. They've had their toy taken away from them," I reported.

I watched as the Arcturians made their case to The Twelve. Although I sensed and saw the anger and confusion of the Arcturian speakers, I was amazed at the calm reserve of their argument. By looking at their features and listening to their words, I might have missed the anger they held in check to maintain their regal composure. I could not miss the subtext of their message, however, because it, too, had a physical shape. Like a hologram, the argument took the form of a 3D model, at least from my vantage point. As the argument shifted, the model changed to reflect the shift.

"And they know," I chuckled. "They know. They're just not ready to say it yet," I said. "They know that the guidance is right; they know that peace is stronger."

The intelligence and capabilities of the Arcturians allowed them to view the result of the interaction with The Twelve before they had finished their argument. They could sense a future where they would not need weapons— even their best ones—because they would have learned to use the power of their vibrations fully and completely to eliminate any breaches in the peace throughout the parts of the universes they were called on to safeguard. While they were tackling submission to what they knew would eventually come, the other group of Stellars pushed them to "stand tall."

"But the smaller," I said referring to the other group of Stellars, "the smaller ones have very broad heads, more flat, but like jowls," I said adding a physical description by holding my hands open on either side of my jaw. "They have thick skin. Really thick skin. They're kind of the negotiators, and they're pushing the Arcturians to stand their ground," I explained. "But, you know, the Arcturians are really smart. So they know when to fight, and they know when *not* to fight, and they know they don't have a chance against The Twelve," I said and, then, laughed. "And The Twelve won't fight anyway. They're more powerful, and that's the point of it. That's the point of the meeting," I said. "The Twelve are showing them to radiate compassion, hope, peace, joy, humility. That's where the strength is."

Feeling the radiance of the vibrations coming from The Twelve was more powerful than the word *powerful* can adequately convey. Nothing seemed to matter. None of the problems seemed important. We—the Stellars and their slightly less disoriented earth visitor—were awash in the rainbow of pulsations that emanated from them. The archangels magnified the intensity, almost as if they were transmitter towers. While the Twelve did not need the archangels, the archangels broadcast the vibrations of The Twelve across the universes. All negativity, all fear, every worry or care bowed to the positive power of the radiance; all the separate vibrations that emanated from The Twelve joined into one single powerful vibration: love. Like the color spectrum in which white represents the amalgamation of all colors, the combination of each of The Twelve's separate vibrations into love created the Divine White Light that protects and nourishes and guides us in our physical manifestations.

"I don't know if it's my filter as a human, but I recognize some of the same dynamics at the Stellar level," I said. "The Pleiadeans are related to the Arcturians. Very close," I said referring to a third group of Stellars. "But the Arcturians have a sense of *entitlement*, I think is the right word. It's subtle; it's not like it is here on earth, but the Pleiadeans have a response to it. It's subtle, too, but it's still a response. It's not so much unlike what we experience here; it's just more subtle, less invasive to the organism," I said. "Because we're all reading from the same story," I tried to explain. "And now I feel the vibration from the Arcturians has changed."

"Are they getting taller?" Douglas asked.

"Yeah," I responded. "And their natural vibration is *physical*. It's physical. You can see the vibration in this dimension," I said. "They know. It's so pleasant to be around them," I said referring to the Arcturians and their peace vibration. "Though," I said as an aside, "they were a little piqued that an earth being would be so judgmental of them. But actually they're being insulting to me because they said if *I* noticed it, it *must* have been true," I laughed. "They're kind of interesting. They're separate physical beings, but they have a link to each other. Developed over millennia," I explained. "You know in ancient Sparta, when they used to do the phalanx? Where they'd come together and put their shields together? This is the Arcturians, except that it's not a physical connection like the Spartans. They can be galaxies away and still feel the connection. It's a phalanx," I announced. "It's really . . . it's really cool."

As I discussed the Arcturians formation into a phalanx, I was struck by how it was both protective and defensive. Each individual Arcturian radiates a peace vibration, just as every earth being radiates joy and others radiate the vibration gifted to them by The Twelve. In the Arcturian version of the Spartan phalanx, the individual vibrations of the members are magnified a hundred or a thousand or a million-fold, and peace is projected out and across the universes through them. Every sentient being, whether they're aware of it or not, are affected by what the Arcturians do in phalanx formation just as every sentient being is affected by the vibrations coming from the archangels who capture and magnify the broadband of love emanating from The Twelve. *As above,* I felt The Twelve express, *so below,* and as The Twelve radiated their fused vibration, the archangels followed suit, and the Arcturians, in some kind of cosmic push, built their phalanx to radiate peace. *As above, so below,* I heard over and over again as the tension that had torn through the Stellar worlds decreased.

In the moment of such powerful vibration when all the beings were adding their own unique vibrations to the Divine White Light of love, I realized the Astrals had succeeded in limiting the phalanx that humans would use to unite in joy; in doing so, they left humans vulnerable without a strong protective and defensive natural shield. By injecting hate into our DNA, they caused division, something completely alien to our systems. *As above, so below* had been disrupted at the cell level, pushing earth beings further and further from Source. With hate, the Astrals stoked division, and kept humans from uniting in joy. The joy vibration of the united was disrupted, and while it was still palpable at the individual level, its magnification potential was all but snuffed out.

At first, the Astrals recognized their success in such manipulation and were proud. But along the way, they lost control of the experiment. Hate and division grew exponentially in the human population, and as the Astrals mingled and reproduced and, fell in love with members of the earth family, some of the succeeding generations of Astrals had a reason to reverse the destruction that earlier generations had encouraged. Their intervention only compounded the problem. Although their intentions were just, the new manipulation of human DNA only created more separation from Source. And now both human and Astral survival were hanging in the balance. The message was meant to restore the phalanx to humanity and, with its restoration, change its course from one of annihilation to one of membership in building and radiating the Divine White Light across universes.

As the vibrations of The Twelve, the archangels, the Arcturians, and all other races bathed me in glorious Divine love, I was given the opportunity to relive the millennia-long history from both the Astral and the human side. It took only seconds for a full reckoning, and the Federation representatives recognized the fundamental truth in the message I had received in the third session. Although they accepted the truth of what I heard and spoke, they would not be able to fully abide by it, at least at first. They would have to work at it, but they knew they would.

"Things have settled," I announced. "The Twelve and the archangels just vibrate. There's nothing that they're saying yet, but the vibration has calmed everybody," I explained. "The fear is gone; you can't see it now."

There was a long silence as I processed what was happening in the Stellar world. As for the tense meeting, The Twelve had already known the outcome—had always known the outcome. They used their linked vibration to encourage the sentient actors to search for what was hidden deep in the very DNA of their souls. They looked for something they had always known, at least at the soul level, and they could feel it bubbling to the surface, almost visible, nearly tangible as love overwhelmed their senses. Truth. It was the essence of the shared, pure language that had brought the disparate multilingual worlds of the Federation together, and it was found in the emanation of The Twelve.

"The archangels are chanting," I said for lack of a better word. "I don't know how else to explain it; it's soothing. The vibration of humility is coming from over here," I said waving my left hand to the left.

In the hypnotic state, I was seeing a small group of ships in the formation of Federation ships. I felt the vibration, saw the vibration, experienced it in every cell in my body.

"Not from the archangels?" Douglas asked.

"No," I responded.

"Is it coming from The Twelve?"

"No. Well yes," I said revising my original answer. "But one of The Twelve is humility."

"Yeah, right," Douglas agreed.

"But these are the beings that radiate that vibration," I said, once again pointing to the left. "I can't understand the name," I admitted. "It's a lot of consonants together, and I...."

"What is the name you're having trouble deciphering?"

"The humility vibrators," I answered.

"Okay."

"It's a different feel—humility," I said. "Different from what we feel here. There's an honesty that goes with the humility vibration. There's an honesty in humility. It just is," I tried to explain.

The vibration was so clear, so unsullied by physical interpretation. There was no deception in it. No false humility. No mediated meekness or modesty. It was simply an accounting of the personal based on pure, unadulterated integrity. Together with the peace vibration of the Arcturians, the humility vibration worked to clarify the intent and mission of the physical participants who stood in the Divine majesty of The Twelve.

"The Twelve, they're ascended masters," I said again. "They're very close to Source," I said awed by the spectacle. "They create. They help to create the planets. They don't do the hard work of it," I clarified. "They do the conceptualization. Well," I corrected myself, "that's hard work too. They do the conceptualizing, but the physical labor is done by others," I explained.

As I discussed the creation aspect of The Twelve with Douglas, I watched the creation of a planet. I *experienced* the creation from all aspects of every participant. Like an experiment in a Petri dish, worlds were created as classrooms with certain lessons in mind. Like a history classroom is imbued with the posters, books, and artifacts of history and an English classroom has the posters, books, and artifacts of English, so too are new worlds purposed with specific lessons in mind. A vibration is assigned to it by one of The Twelve. The vibration corresponds to an individual member of The Twelve who calculates the effect and necessity of the vibration to the universes. Each distinct part of the new world—the physical beings with souls, the animals, the plant-life, the colors and sounds and make-up are determined prior to its creation. Each part has a role to play in the lesson to be experienced on the planet, and each part is created with care and instilled with love through the emanation of Divine White Light.

In the *Talmud,* there is a verse that says *every blade of grass has an angel that bends over it and whispers,* Grow! Grow! This is the truth of creation. There are no mistakes. There are no wrong turns. With mathematical precision, each distinct part of the new creation is assigned to a caretaker. Sometimes the caretaker is an angel; sometimes it is assigned to a physical entity. All are part of Source. In the case of earth, the Astrals—Stellars originally—were assigned to safeguard the new and naïve population: humans. At some point, however, the Astrals' free will enabled them to reassign some of our essential being to better serve them. In wanting to harness the joy emanation for themselves, the Astrals set themselves and the population they were tasked with safeguarding on a collision course. And now we find ourselves at the apex of that path.

"All the Stellars have sent congregations to share the message. They have *not* invited the Astrals," I said with particular emphasis and a little judgement on *not.* "They are beginning to realize that they live the story of the Astrals. Not always. Certainly not as much as the humans. But enough," I said.

"The Stellars are realizing that?" Douglas asked.

"Yes. They're confused," I added. "They can accept that they do this, but they cannot understand how to stop doing it. Now if they vibrate correctly, they recognize the truth in the message. They recognize the power in their own vibrations," I explained. "And while they're not ready to give up the ideas they formed over millennia, they do, at least, recognize that they must."

"I'm sorry; that they must?" Douglas prompted.

"Give up the story they participated in."

"Okay. Thank you," Douglas responded.

"They must break free, and it will take time. The Arcturians are radiating a strong peace throughout the universes now," I told Douglas. "They want us to tell them how to win. And even in saying it, they realize their mistake. 'How do we let go?' they asked."

A Message from The Twelve: Like a Fish in Water who Finally Notices Water

Jasmine stepped in mid-conversation, "There is fear of the unknown. There is fear of the *other*," she said, clearly establishing herself.

When Jasmine emerged, my speech became more deliberate. Slower. Less choppy. She did not waste words; instead, each word was considered for its impact.

"And the *other* refers to humans?" Douglas asked.

"To whomever we categorize as *other*," Jasmine responded.

"Mm," Douglas said, recognizing the entrance of one of The Twelve. "So not part of?" Douglas trailed off.

"Not part of *your* story," she finished for him.

"Right."

"Your story is two stories now. That's your personal conflict," she explained to Douglas. "It is why in general a soul that comes in two parts does not have contact. You have competing stories," Jasmine said.

"Hope and peace, is that right?" Douglas asked referring to vibrations.

"Yes, but you have a conflict with your peace vibration from the Arcturians and the joy vibration here on the earth which is do-able," Jasmine admitted. "But you have a *story* that has been written by the Arcturians which cast the Astrals as the *other*," she said clarifying the real conflict for Douglas.

As Jasmine spoke, I came to understand that Astrals were once primarily Arcturians and Pleiadeans with a small smattering of other Stellar groups represented. In other words, Astrals were Stellars. The mission-driven mindset of the Arcturians made it easier for rogue members to manipulate the human race for, as they told themselves, the betterment of all involved. But it was far from better for either side. Especially in the long run. The rogue group worked to harness the joy vibration with the least amount of harm to its hosts: humans. They never admitted to having selfish and self-centered reasons for such action, and as it became obvious the experiment was failing, they hunkered down and tried harder to make it work. Forgetting about the self-interested genesis of their actions acted as a salve for their misguided and, ultimately, disastrous intrusions into humanity's vibratory phalanx. In the whitewashing of their mission, they told themselves it was done to protect humanity from itself, and to assuage their guilt, they built a story around the otherness of human beings.

"Here on earth, there are other *others*, and you can think of them as local *others*. Those who are different from you," Jasmine explained. "But you can handle this, or we would not have given you the gift. And it is why when sometimes you're connecting with your other part of your soul, you feel the pull. You feel a much more comfortable existence with him because you find the peace vibration," she said.

For a few minutes, my ego returned even as I stood in the vibration of The Twelve, the archangels, the Arcturians, and the myriad other races. I felt jealous of Douglas, I am embarrassed to admit now, who had learned so much about his soul base.

I want to know, I whined. *Tell me where I'm from*, I asked.

"She wants to know about the Pleiades," Jasmine told Douglas, "but it's not time for that. First, she needs to connect to the story. Then, she needs to connect to the message. Then, we can tell her about the Pleiades," Jasmine explained. "She's more at home on earth than you because her essence is the joy vibration, so on earth, she feels the joy vibration. She is still conflicted though because she is not of this soul base," Jasmine explained. "So, she sees now what the vibration of the Pleiades is," she laughed at my deduction. "It is joy, and they've had a special relationship with humanity because of the shared vibration." Jasmine changed course, "it's odd that they fear us—the Stellars. They have a sense of awe, but that awe translates a bit into fear."

"And who is it they fear?" Douglas asked.

"The Twelve."

"Oh. Okay."

"The archangels," she added. "Like humans, they recognize a boundary between the physical and the spiritual," she said referring to the Stellars. "Their boundaries are much more fluid than humanity's. They know we are real, but they still fear. A little bit. If the planet survives, humanity will evolve to this as well," Jasmine said. "The veil between the here and the hereafter will be gone or, at least, thinner."

I was given a glimpse of earth's potential evolution, and its movement to higher and higher dimensions, its ability to communicate more fluidly with the spiritual realm, its reconnection to Source. I was confused because I had also seen the destruction of the earth.

I thought . . ., I said before being cut off.

This is just one of the paths for humans that depend on your success.

Jasmine meant *your* in the collective sense, I was relieved to know.

"You may ask," Jasmine told Douglas after a long silence.

"Was that an invitation?" Douglas asked.

"Yes."

"Okay."

"Feel the peace. Feel the peace vibration at your soul," Jasmine instructed Douglas. "It will guide you. They are waiting."

"Yes, I understood that," Douglas replied. "So, let me tell you what I've been thinking," Douglas began, "as you're sketching this out in the last few weeks, I get so caught up in the content—in the detail—of your sketching. But my mind says *this is all great and good, but what has to change?*"

"Oh," Jasmine responded positively to the question. "Wow! Wouldn't it be easy if I told you that part?" Jasmine joked.

"Well, I can tell you that my mind goes there because I'm always looking for that bigger picture. I get that you'll keep sketching it out, but *okay, now what*?" Douglas asked.

"And now it's your free will to figure out the path," she responded, rather too simply or cryptically. "And Golodor," she said referring to Douglas' Arcturian mate, "is quite proud that you asked the question that everyone thought. Yes," Jasmine smiled before continuing, "he says *no pressure*."

"Yeah," Douglas laughed in response. "I appreciate that thought. Now let me just get clear. You said *my free will* will find the path. Who's free will? Who's the *my*?"

"Your free will. Golodor's free will. Her free will. Collective," Jasmine answered with examples. In doing so, she clarified the doctrine of free will; it is both individual and collective.

"Oh, so it's on the three of us?" Douglas asked.

"It's on the whole universe to make the change. All universes," she clarified. "You've developed awareness like a fish in water," she tried to explain. "A fish doesn't recognize water until it's taken *out* of water. Now you've been taken out of your story. You will find a way now. Collectively, there's enough of you that you can find a way," she explained. "Yes, and now there'll be more work between the soul bases. Different Stellars will work more with humanity through this message. They have been blocked," she told Douglas. "They have been blocked by humanity from helping."

"They've been blocked by what?" Douglas asked.

"By fear," she responded.

"Okay. Okay. I get that."

"Mm," she agreed.

"That is loud and clear. What just shifted to ... I'll use a simple word ... to *decrease* the fear?"

"You are the fish that has been taken out of water," Jasmine connected her metaphor to the collective, "and now your job and the other lightworkers with you is to take the other fish out of water as well. Once you recognize your circumstance, you can change it. You can rewrite your story," she pronounced. "Today there will be a disruption. You'll feel it. The vibrations are so strong throughout the universes right now," she informed Douglas. "The Twelve vibrate. The archangels vibrate, and all the Stellars are vibrating their natural vibration. And you will see a change on the earth today. You will see an effect of the vibration," she said. "It may not last, but it will have an effect. Some of it will be a fight against the vibration, and that's often the most visible result. Sometimes it's physical on the environment, and sometimes it's obvious between people standing their ground, refusing to budge, refusing to open their eyes. But you will also see change in those who will accept the vibration."

"I'm working with the story piece that you cast out clearly to be understood, and up to today, I thought *yes, this story and the twist from the story as I thought about it,* and suddenly it changed today and became contemporaneous. It was no longer in the olden days or in the future, but suddenly it was now."

"Yes," she replied, "and all is now."

"Working on that."

"You cast everything in present, past, future, but realize we don't have those constraints."

"But it ...."

"But you live a human existence," she finished his sentence for him.

"I've been told that."

Both Jasmine and Douglas laughed.

"I look in the mirror every day," Douglas joked.

"We can assure you," Jasmine carried on the joke.

"Do you understand?" Douglas asked Jasmine, referring to his confusion.

"Yes, I do. Let me try to help you."

"I mean I get what you're saying about time," Douglas said, "but all of a sudden, this had. . . I mean what I'm tracking is all the Stellars came."

"Yes."

"The Arcturians came," Douglas continued.

"They're still here," Jasmine corrected.

"No. I get that. The point is they came to this nexus point . . .."

"Yes."

"To have clarity . . .."

"Yes."

"About what was said."

"Yes," Jasmine assured. "They have not all accepted."

"I bet not," Douglas added.

"They understand," Jasmine continued, "that it is the truth, but often we understand the truth and have a hard time getting to there."

"Okay," Douglas agreed.

"And it will take some time, and that's okay. But they will find a way to get there, and they know this," Jasmine assured Douglas. "They know this."

"So why did The Twelve choose this venue to share this . . . I don't even have an adjective or word . . . this . . . to deliver this profound message?"

"Yes, you mean this office or . . . ?"

"No. No," he said and, then, changed his mind. "Maybe I do in part," Douglas relented.

"Mm."

"Maybe there's a piece that I'm like *why is this happening here*?" Douglas chuckled.

"Yes. You are one of many. You are one of many."

"Okay."

"You are one of many," she said looking to alleviate the pressure on Douglas.

"That are getting the same messages?"

"Yes."

"At the same time?"

"Yes. And I want to clarify a story for you so that maybe this will help you accept. You know, you no longer doubt that you had a soul mission before you were born into this existence. Am I right?"

"Yes," Douglas responded.

"You also knew you came to this earth not fully aware of that mission. Is that right?" she asked.

"Mm-hmm."

"And that your job in this human experience was to find this mission. Yes?"

"Hmm," Douglas sighed. "Okay."

"Yes, and you strayed from the path and moved back on the path and circled the path and went backwards on the path, but you," Jasmine pointed out, "have found part of your mission. Yes? Would you agree?"

"I'll go with that."

"It is the same with the story. The story now you know. There is a story that's been written *for* you, in part, and written *by* you, in part, and now you need to find a way to rewrite your story."

"Okay," Douglas voiced his understanding.

"Just like finding your mission," Jasmine completed the circle; "you didn't always know consciously that you had a mission. You knew somewhere inside you that you had a mission, and right now you know inside you, as do the Stellars, that there is truth in rewriting or the need to rewrite the story, and you will struggle to find that path," she said. "And there's a reason for that struggle. The struggle connects you to the new story, just as your struggle connected you to mission. And it is your greatest gift," she assured Douglas, "to have free will. At any time you can choose *not* to follow your mission, and at any time, you can choose to live in the story that you are living, but you will not because now that you're aware, you will move forward."

"And was this built into my soul contract?" Douglas asked.

"The story?"

"No, the rewriting of the story."

"Yes. Not your soul contract personally, but your collective soul contract. So if you understand your soul contract, that's your mission level, but the story is a collective contract, and you have a collective contract with other soul beings. The outcome is not determined," Jasmine said referring to Douglas' collective soul contract, "but the goal has been contracted."

"To save humanity?" Douglas asked.

"I'm sorry."

"To save humanity?" Douglas repeated.

"Yes. The story must be rewritten to save humanity. The story must be rewritten to save the Astrals. They have blinders on—same as an animal; they cannot see outside of their story, and until today, you, the Stellars, others did not know you had your blinders on."

"Right."

"And now you must do the same for the Astrals and for the humans."

"Oh. Yippie Kei Yay," Douglas said sarcastically.

"Yes. It's exciting, not?" Jasmine joked in response.

"Yes," Douglas answered. "When I get there beyond my anxiety."

"It is part of the process."

"Apparently, I didn't want to get bored," Douglas joked.

"You didn't take this existence lightly. You struggled," she said. "It was a long time before you accepted."

"I can't take the legal position that I signed under duress?" Douglas joked.

"No duress. But you know that," she laughed. "Maybe a little peer pressure. No duress."

"Oh my."

"She didn't want this either. She still doesn't want it," Jasmine said referring to me.

"Yeah. I get that. I got that. But I have to keep asking the same question: what in the world did I sign on for?"

"There is a sense—whether you fail or you succeed in this existence on your mission—of the great good you are doing. Your soul is growing at an incredible rate having chosen this. Hers, too," she added. "Others too. And you can see it. You can measure against the regular person, the regular human and recognize your soul has grown so far. There has been a lifting."

"I'm sorry," Douglas interjected; "what was the last word?"

"There has been a lifting."

"Oh. *Lifting.*"

"And you know this," Jasmine said.

"It's hard sometimes to sort between hubris and reality," Douglas explained.

"Ahh," Jasmine exclaimed; "and so that's why the humility vibration was sent."

"Mm."

"Humility is not how you conceive of it here on the earth. It's honesty."

"Pure honesty," Douglas added.

"Pure honesty."

"Yes."

"Honesty with yourself," Jasmine added.

"Yes. I get that."

"I love the sunrise in Africa," Jasmine said; "that had nothing to do with the message," she laughed.

"But it's pure," Douglas added.

"Yes," she whispered in response. "It is a beautiful site. If you have not seen it, you should," she told Douglas.

Although I wanted to participate, once again, with Jasmine as she applied a human experience to the physical creation of the earth, I could not. I felt dizzy, disoriented, a little nauseous. After I had arrived, I had been given an injection of some sort that allowed me to participate at a basic level in the Stellar's dimension. I had never fully acclimated, but as the injection wore off, I found myself more and more fatigued, more and more unsettled.

I had crawled under a non-physical ledge on the Stellar ship—more of a *shadow* of a ledge really—and curled up in the fetal position. My eyes were closed; my forearms cradling my face, and I waited to be sent back. This time I *longed* to be sent back to earth.

"She will not be able to stay much longer in this dimension," Jasmine said, referring to me.

"Oh. Okay."

"It hurts her, but you can have a few more questions."

"Well, let's see," Douglas settled in. "It is interesting to look at that Arcturian anthology and see it as a story."

"The book that she read?"

"The book that she started to read. Yes," Douglas said.

"She cannot read it yet," Jasmine warned.

"Yes. But I understand that, in fact, it is the Arcturian story."

"Yes," Jasmine answered.

"Yes."

"But you know this; you don't need to read the book. You read the book to qualify what you already knew."

"It would seem so," Douglas conceded. "So the—I'm calling him my twin—because he won't give me a name. There's a reason, I'm sure."

"Mm-hmm."

"But, anyway, so I've been calling him Douglas 1."

"Your birth name is a misplaced earth name," Jasmine chimed in.

"Mm."

"She has a hard time writing it; every time she types *Douglas*, she types it wrong. Every time."

"And that's because?" Douglas led.

"It's not your true name."

"Yes."

"But I cannot tell you. Not yet."

"Okay," Douglas relented. "And," Douglas began again before being cut off by Jasmine.

"Because you share an existence. What we reveal about your soul is revealed about the other, and that disrupts free will."

"Interesting," Douglas sighed. "Oh, so what you're saying is that if I knew the Arcturian's name, I would understand it is my name?"

"Yes. And he would understand as well. He is not as aware. He knows there's something interesting about an earth being, but he is not as aware. The more you know," she explained to Douglas, "the more you transmit automatically to him."

"Mm."

"Or her. Arcturians. You have assumed *him*," Jasmine corrected.

"I get that. So who . . . who is the other representative from Arcturus to the intergalactic Federation?"

"You don't need to know yet," she responded.

"Okay."

"The only reason you know one name is because he has a special connection to you."

"Mm-hmm," Douglas agreed. "Then who's been showing up on the ship with Golodor, then, if it's not that aspect from Arcturus because he doesn't have that . . . or he or she doesn't have that awareness."

"Ah-hah," Jasmine understood. "Has some awareness of a connection, but not at the level of connection that you know right now. He will however because you know."

"Right."

"There are many that are on the ship with Golodor when you're there, but you have the problem with dimension, too," she explained referring to the disorientation I had been feeling during the whole of the session. "It's very hard to notice detail."

"Yes," Douglas agreed.

"But you're looking at just one other person? Yes?"

"Yes."

"The reason we hesitate to give you names is because you draw attention to them on the Astral plane. There'll be time," she assured Douglas, "but it's only when your mind is stronger against Astral influence."

"Mm."

"Does that make sense?"

"No."

Both laugh as Jasmine added, "*this* is humility." After a short pause, she said, "I asked him if it's okay." After another short silence, Jasmine responded, "he said, 'soon.'"

"Okay,"

"He is not Arcturian though."

"I'm sorry. I lost context here. Who's the *he*?" Douglas asked.

"The other. The . . . not *friend* to Golodor. The . . . ."

"Oh, I got it," Douglas said.

"The supervisor to Golodor," Jasmine finished.

"Okay."

"He is not Arcturian."

"Ah, that's my confusion," Douglas replied. "Okay."

"But very similar," she added. "Yes, she knows now," Jasmine said in reference to my understanding of the other's origin. "Yes, she knows," she said again.

I understood that Golodor's supervisor was Pleiadean. He checked on me regularly as, at first I participated on board the ship and, later after the injection began to wear off, I succumbed to the fetal position. I recognized him, knew his soul, but could not place his name.

We were together. Before. In another life, he assured me.

When he laid his hands on me, the trembling that had overtaken me, stopped. Like Reiki on steroids, his touch calmed me, healed me. He was kind, compassionate, and I felt the joy vibration radiating from him.

"And what is it she knows?" Douglas asked.

"The other is Pleiadean," Jasmine answered.

"Mmm."

"He's gentle."

"Mm-hmm."

"And the Golodor, because he has a connection to you, is not as gentle with you as the other is, and it's a good balance for you."

"Mm-hmm," Douglas agreed.

"You've been to the Pleiades," she announced, "in a soul life."

"Mm-hmm," Douglas agreed as if the comment were normal. "I thought so."

"Mm. Many times, and as an Arcturian, you visit," she added. "You have a pull to the planet, and you'll dream about it in the next few weeks. You'll remember. That will be our gift," Jasmine smiled.

"That will be fun," Douglas accepted.

"I just . . . as a side comment just so you know . . . not that you don't . . . with all that's going on here, I'm having a little trouble figuring out who I am anymore," Douglas admitted.

"Mm."

"I suppose that's a good thing."

"No. It's confusing as a human, but you are a soul having a human existence. You are much more expansive than Douglas. And you know this, but what you are struggling with is being constrained in a vessel so small for your soul," Jasmine soothed.

"Mm."

"And the more we bring awareness to it, the more you'll grapple with that, and yet you'll find a place to be okay with it."

"Well that's good. I was worried there would really be something to look forward to," Douglas said.

"No," she laughed.

"So the name *Douglas* constrains me?"

"Yes."

"I get it."

"I think you had another name. Another earth name."

"Oh."

"She is like a daisy wilting," Jasmine said noticing me in the fetal position in the other dimension. "She must," she laughed; "she must come back."

"Okay. I will," Douglas said.

"She cannot," Jasmine said still laughing; "she cannot be in this dimension."

"All right," Douglas said. "Thanks for the most exciting, interesting day, and we will chat again, I'm sure."

"Yes," Jasmine said brightly; "and you will be granted the dream, and Golodor says it won't be long until you see him as well. He's letting you know, as a joke, that when we put you on the spot for questions, all of the Stellars were listening, and you did fine."

"Yeah," Douglas laughed. "For a human."

"Well," Jasmine laughed, "and this is what *he* said," she said. "Yes, I will have Michael escort her; she is done."

"Thank you."

After a long silence, I re-entered Douglas' office in the physical world, "Oof," I said to mark the feeling of the other dimension.

"Yes. She said you were fried," Douglas said in sympathy.

It took nine days to finally put the finishing touches on the chapter. I fought it in every cell of my body. I did not want to write it; I did not want to re-experience the pain of being in the Stellar dimension, and I certainly did not want to write about intergalactic life. Of course, it was my choice. Always my choice. Writing this chapter was a trial I had to choose to survive, and I did. Both choose and survive, I mean.

You overcame it, Jasmine whispered.

And as the next session with Douglas hovered in the very near future, I felt the presence of Michael as an almost constant companion; I heard Jasmine more regularly and without the need for hypnosis, and sometimes I felt a gift vibration from one of The Twelve. It was always the right vibration, just when I needed it most.

Archangel Gabriel had been reading over my shoulder as I wrote, and a trusted friend-writer gave me the gift of reading the chapters and making me feel normal. "There's a certain logic to it," she said of the message, and I realized, at some point, that part of her mission was to make sure I stayed on mine. She is the much better-looking, much more intelligent Samwise Gamgee to my frumpier Frodo, I guess.

As I finished the chapter, I looked out to the Rockies off in the distance and saw the abundant white clouds in the blue-blue of the mile-high sky, and I whispered my thanks for the experience. At least for now.

ACT V

Learning from a Past Life

25 June 2019

When my soul nods to me like some chance passerby
And walks off in the rain—hear me out:
Your earth, oh, my Lord God, is splendid, it's true,
But I'd better come out and be there inside.
~Olga Sedakova

Intuition's Call to Action was Strong When I Actually Listened

Dwell on the beauty of life. Watch the stars,
and see yourself running with them.
~Marcus Aurelius

Intuition is a curious thing, often at its clearest when we least expect it. Because we are so often surprised by it and its strength, we choose to disregard the guidance that accompanies it. It is not an easy choice; intuition's call to action is strong. In an attempt to resolve the persistent, aching, gnawing feeling that comes with *in*action, we begin to deny the accuracy of intuition; we question its authenticity. We focus on its lack of logic. We content ourselves with its apparent flaws and choose to face issues, choices, events, needs, and necessities without any guidance at all. Without help. We teach ourselves that it is better this way, and our overly rational society reflects this great untruth back to us. In other words, we tune out our gut-burning intuition because, we are taught, it is not rational. Intuition is not objective. Yet, of course, it's not objective. It's not supposed to be.

Intuition forces us to see with the soul, not the mind. The very nature of intuition lays in its instinctual knowingness, its understanding without the need for conscious reasoning. We know because we know, in other words. Logic, reason, and rationality have nothing to do with it; it is the very absence of these things that makes intuition ... well ... intuition. And it comes in many forms: a simple knowing, a feeling in the pit of the stomach, a strong reaction to or for something, an irrational fear. For me, when Douglas placed me in a hypnotic state, the pull of the purely logical was weakened. Although it reared its head from time to time, hypnosis allowed the overly rational part of me to take its place behind the gift of intuition, and I could hear and see and feel and experience the guidance of spirit, the archangels, and The Twelve.

Each hypnotic session began on the first step of floating stairs. At the top stood a door and around the door, I saw the blue of the sky. There were no walls. No anchors for the steps. No frame for the door. In fact, there was no sky. I had created it all—not consciously, of course—to help make the transition to the spirit world more palatable to my human mind. Filtered light through clouds illuminated the end of the climb. Sometimes the light shone brighter because the steps getting to the top were enveloped in an absolute, inky darkness, but not because there was anything to fear. Rather, darkness helped to disorient and, then, quiet my ego. There were times when my climb to the top was shrouded in blackness, but a radiant pure light poured through the treads. The light was never harsh, never cold; instead, it was alive with spirit touch. It sizzled and snapped, and as I walked from the here to the hereafter, a steady stream of noncorporeal hands held me and guided me, caressed me and wrapped me in love of all kinds: a mother's love, the love of a child, a friend, a soulmate, the butterflies-in-the belly love of first love, the birth of a baby love, the feel of a father's warm, whiskery cheek kind of love, the love of new-won freedom and the love of stillness, of being at peace, of all is right in the world kind of love. Infinite varieties of love. Infinite. Michael, the archangel, the protector, the emanator of all vibrations, walked with me to the door to the hereafter. Always. And from time to time, he invited others to join us on the trek.

With my eyes closed in physical space, I pictured myself taking each step at the exact moment that Douglas called out the number to which it corresponded. "Six. Deeper. Deeper," Douglas called, and I would take the sixth step. After a few sessions, I knew the routine, but I continued to follow Douglas' count. Then, I could enjoy each step by stopping and noticing the gifts that waited for me: sometimes another archangel, a beautiful image, animals, a memory, a song, poetry, a loved one in spirit. Since the time in hypnotic space stretches and shifts and vanishes into no-thing-ness, I might spend hours or days on each step as I waited for Douglas.

In our fifth session, there was a long silence as I stood stubbornly next to the archangels—Michael and Gabriel—and debated about whether or not I should open the door to my spiritual space. The count that took me up the floating steps to the door was hurried; Douglas wasn't messing around, but as we reached the top, I stopped and waited for his direction to open the door. He had always given the command before.

It's okay, Michael nodded at the door. *You may open it.*

He didn't say to, I said referring to Douglas' instructions.

You're here now, Michael explained. He was not angry; he was amused by my reticence. Gabriel was amused at our discussion.

We waited for a very long time, me giggling at what I understood was foolishness on my part, Michael nodding the okay to open the door. While it was an eternity of waiting on the staircase, it was only a matter of minutes in earth time. Still, it was a long time. As we stood waiting, staring at the door, I became aware that the door had no real frame, no knob. It was an image of a door, nothing more. But it was an image so real, so physical that it felt like a door to me. As I stood firm in my refusal to enter, I was keenly aware that the door was only a metaphor. It was a way for me to differentiate between the world of my reality and the world of hypnosis.

Well, ask him, Michael urged.

I looked to Gabriel for confirmation that Michael's idea was a good one. I sensed his smile and nod of the head.

The Fifth Hypnotic Session: Meeting the Me of Another Lifetime

"Michael asked for you to open the door for me," I laughed at the absurdity; "I'm a rule follower."

"So, open the door," Douglas said. "Step through. Close it behind you, and step into your sacred space."

"And he said to joke with you about the quick count," I complied referring to the rapid-fire lead up to the hypnotic state. Douglas laughed.

"It's really beautiful where I am," I said in a wistful voice although I had not yet figured out where I stood. "Michael is radiating a lilac color," I told Douglas; "it's really calm and soothing today, and he met me on the first step," I said. "And Gabriel joined at three, and Gabriel vibrates blue. Light blue," I added. "I think I'm in a physical place; it's really beautiful."

As I fell further into hypnosis and more in tune with the world I was experiencing, my voice grew distant, less connected to the physical realm of earth. I was taking in the beauty of my surroundings, at once so different from what I knew on earth, but also comfortably similar in terms of features. While the colors and smells and sounds had no resemblance to the earth realm, there were mountains and streams, grass and trees, a sky, a moon. Two in fact. They may have been very different from what I knew, but they were features I recognized. As I stood taking it all in, the unfamiliar became more and more familiar. I knew before I knew where I was.

"The skies are lilac and orange," I began to describe the space. "It's night. I know it's night. There's a huge, huge, huge moon. Right here," I said pointing to the left in physical space. "Almost it's like it's so close that you can," I stopped to regroup; "it looks like it's sitting on the ground of the planet. It's really beautiful," I exhaled. "It's the light source now."

The moon had the brightness and nearness of what we humans call a *harvest moon*. It looked close—*really* close—and in comparison to the relative distance of our moon, this huge moon seemed to consume most of one-third of the sky. While there was a second, smaller moon, it paled in comparison to the first.

"And there's like a monorail," I explained in a far-off voice. "Here," I said tracing a track around my right side. "The colors are something like you would see in a Van Gogh painting," I added trying to describe the juxtaposition of colors in the landscape. "It's a memory," I said with sudden understanding. "It's a gift. They're giving me a gift. It's a memory," I explained. "The dome is spectacular. The stars are here," I said sweeping my arm above my head from left to right. "And they don't have . . .," I stopped to rephrase. "They light with natural light, so it doesn't damage the environment or damage the view. It's spectacular," I said emphatically. "You can see in the heavens . . . in the stars . . . comets. You can see the tails in the sky. Much more often than you would see here."

The night sky moved from pale lilac to the black of space beyond; a shower of comet tails zig-zagged in and around and between the absolute blackness of the night sky and the star shine of the heavens. Between the pale lilac of the bottom-most layer of the sky and the planet's surface, a pale orange added a cushion of color.

"And my family is here," I announced. "Oh, I'm here too," I said, recognizing my soul in another physical existence. "There's a kind of a flatness to the face," I began to describe the look of the people in front of me; "except there are cheekbones, and the face is almost angular, straight, rounds at the chin, but kind of comes like this," I said outlining the face in physical space. "Like a heart. Like almost a heart-shape. I had three children in this life," I announced.

As the realization of what I was seeing hit me, tears began to flow down my cheeks. I was viewing a memory of a past life, but it was happening in a human's concept of real time. I could interact fully in it, not only in the environment but also with the people, including the *me* of a past life. A flood of memory poured through me, infusing every single inch of me with the feeling and thoughts and understandings of a previous life. I relived the past life in only a few seconds of earth time and saw my children being born, the accident that nearly took my husband's life, my sickness at an old age that led to a peaceful, easy death. And I realized that I missed that life and the people and things that were part of it.

"Physically the Pleiadeans look like Arcturians," I said, continuing to act like an observer rather than a participant. "The same general shape. Their faces are different. They're related; they're very close," I said of the two Stellar groups. "There are not as many digits," I said spreading my fingers in front of me. "There's not as many. Feels like maybe three on each hand, but they're different," I said referring to the Pleiadean hand; "they're tapered, and they're . . .," I trailed off.

Only as an observer could I hold my emotions in check, yet as I described what I was experiencing to Douglas, I lost the battle with my emotions as I allowed myself to become a player in the memory. In a display that is reminiscent of a staged family photo on earth, the physical being—the soul-me—had her arm looped around the youngest child. He might have been three years old. My husband from the prior life stood next to me, a little taller, a little more regal in his bearing. Next to their younger brother, two sisters filled out the photo-like still-life. Except they weren't still. They were interacting with each other. And me.

"Oh, I loved this life. This was a good life," I said, choking up with emotion. "The sky is so beautiful; it's lilac. Even at night, it doesn't turn black," I said changing my focus, hoping to change the rising emotion. "There's black above, but it's lilac, and then there's a thin orange-y color," I sniffled. "And it looks like it's over kind of like a mountain; the orange is," I explained. "This was a good life," I repeated.

A long silence ensued as I discussed my mission with the other part of my soul. Hers was the life, I slowly began to understand, where I committed to the mission I face in this one.

We knew it would be hard, she admitted and, as she looked at her husband, he looked at her. Both nodded in agreement. *But there was no other way*, she smiled. *We had to do this.*

Her *we* referred to the *me* of the past life and the *me* of my current earth incarnation. It was a strange feeling to hear such a connection. *We* had found each other across time and space, and *we* recognized the fundamental *me*-ness in each other. *She* like *me* were part of one greater soul. *We* were different incarnations of Jasmine.

Although her voice was not physical, I heard it as a pleasant tingling pulsation. Almost chime-like. Or more like a voice with a crystalline structure. The sound entered and rippled down my body as we interacted, and I was very aware that, with her voice, my nerve endings tingled in tandem, excitedly, almost alive.

"I have a kind of dog in this life, but it's not a dog. And I even baked about which the archangels are making fun of me. They say I've gotten lazy," I laughed out loud.

There is a happiness—always a happiness—when I interact with the archangels. They do not have the capacity to be negative; instead, they help physical beings avoid negativity by radiating out their vibration. In so doing, we, in turn, begin to radiate our own vibration, blunting and eventually replacing any lingering sense of negativity.

"And you're here," I announced to Douglas; "in a past life."

"Mmm," he responded.

"You're an Arcturian in this life," I assured him. "The Pleiades are beautiful and so you come to visit. It doesn't take long," I said. "There's a way that the Arcturians can come without being in a ship. They," I hesitated as it was explained to me. "Oh, like what I was explaining before to you. They can . . .."

"Teleport," Douglas finished.

"Yeah. Teleport, but not like the movies. Not like *Star Trek* when they do that thing," I said mimicking the way the officers of the Enterprise teleported.

"Right," Douglas agreed.

"It's more of an image," I tried to explain the concept more fully. "They can forward an image to another place, and yet they have the same physical property that they do on their own planet," I said recognizing the ability of the Arcturians to feel physical sensations even as an image. "But they are still on their own planet; this is just a fully physical, holistic image that they project onto something else, and it's amazing because they can feel and . . . like . . . they'll still eat on the new planet. And they'll wash, and they'll experience life the same way, but it's just an image," I explained. "We can go to Arcturus, too," I said, referring to the Pleiadeans. "But the traffic usually goes one way," I laughed. "To the Pleiades."

Douglas laughed too. I knew Douglas was waiting for more about his role in this past life.

I had begun to feel fully a part of the memory I was experiencing. I had recovered the feelings, thoughts, and dreams of a prior life while the feelings, thoughts, and dreams of my current life stayed intact. There did not seem to be any contradiction in holding both at the same time; rather, it was natural. At some level, my soul had already incorporated the memories of the past life with those of my current life and, in fact, with all the memories of all other lives. Like different episodes in one particular life, the different episodes of all lives lived comfortably integrated with each other, even when the episodes may have contradicted the feelings or meanings of others.

"They knew in this life that this life was coming," I told him and, then, deliberately switched to the *we* pronoun. "We knew in the life I'm seeing that this life was coming in human form," I explained. "And although time doesn't mean the same thing there, I would put this just after the time of Jesus," I said referring to the memory I was experiencing. "It doesn't feel that long ago," I said a little sadly.

A significant silence ensued as I relived a few of the happy memories I had in the life I was visiting. In one scene, I experienced a type of laughter that shook my whole body as I watched my then-children rolling down a hill, not like we do on the earth, but with the same kind of result. On the Pleiades, the atmosphere is different. Physical manifestations do not necessarily touch; instead, there is a small barrier between the make-up of one physical body and the make-up of another. When the children rolled down the hill, this barrier allowed them to gain more speed and be impacted by the changes, bumps, dips in the surface; however, rather than feel physical discomfort, the barrier simply became bigger and the roll was more exciting.

When my children in my current life were younger, we lived in a pretty little community close to Mount Gretna, Pennsylvania. A thinly populated, sylvan-like idyllic environment, we walked a skinny path in the woods to the little Chautauqua where the lake and summer-camp-ish-like houses stood inhabited year-round. On the rare occasions when we drove, we chose the road with a hidden dip. By the time the kids were old enough to know about the dip, I had been enjoying it for years. Although I could not make it out visually, I knew the shape of the trees and the slight turn in the road, and the little bluff before it.

In other words, I knew enough to slow down long before the car encountered the dip, but I did not. Like a child, I let the Volvo station wagon hit the bluff at a moderate speed so that by the time the hidden dip was a reality, we—me, the children, and the poor Volvo—had the temporary weightlessness of being air born. While I knew sailing over the bluff and into the dip this way was not at all a good choice for the car, I never missed a chance to experience that buffer between our physical bodies and the ground, the buoyant, semi-second of freedom from gravity. I told myself it was for the children; now, I believe it might have been more for me to spark a hidden memory of my life on the Pleiades.

"They're giving me the sense of real joy, of what it feels like to unite in joy," I said of the soul-me Pleiadean and her family. "We have that capacity here on earth, and we just never experience it," I said a little sadly. "There's a microcosm of the vibration that can happen at the individual level and the family level and the community level. It builds," I said referring to the levels of joy we can experience. "But there's a *magnificent* vibration at the planet level."

What I felt was a humming sensation of joy. It filled the air with song; it tickled right to the cell level. It expanded and shrunk and expanded again as individuals joined and retreated from the vibration. There was a shared sense of community—planet-wide. There was acceptance, at least much more than we experience here, and differences were just differences, not characteristics to fear. In fact, the variety of characteristics any one individual brought to the planet was simply the mix of elements of who they were physically, nothing else. It was a completely foreign concept to pick one or some of those elements as different enough to fear. Of course, not everyone held the same values and beliefs, and these became the basis for people to disagree with each other, but not because of a change or difference in the physical shell that held their souls.

"And even if you never met someone before, you know them," I sniffed. "There's the connection between souls that's so clear; that's one of the reasons the Arcturians come."

"I'm sorry. They like to come because . . .?" Douglas asked.

"Because they can feel pure connection. Soul-to-soul. So, what the Pleiadeans do really well is they are able to remember their source. They remember who they are. They remember they are souls having a physical experience, and all the Arcturians know that. Archangel Michael says sometimes they're too cerebral to experience it," I said referring to the Arcturians. "It doesn't mean that the Pleiadeans aren't cerebral as well; it's just that for whatever reason, they don't overthink it. Arcturians have a tendency to overthink which is part of what makes them so good at their mission," I said.

The Arcturians are the peacekeepers in the universes, especially the universe where earth is located. They are strategic thinkers. They are hyper-aware of how each decision can have an effect on the outcome of their mission. So, they run out scenario after scenario when faced with a decision in an effort to make the right decision. This strategic thinking is important in regards to their mission, but it has become ingrained in their everyday lives. At times, therefore, it gets in the way of just being.

"The Pleiadean's heart is visible. You can see the heartbeat; you can see the heart. It's in the same place where human hearts are," I explained. "Oh, Arcturians' too. They're kind of telling me that the heart locus is the same for most races, but you can see it in the Pleiadean. It's really soothing like a gentle movement of the heart and just a nice color," I added. "The Pleiadeans are a little more playful than the Arcturians, but that's another reason the Arcturians like to come; it is because they relax a little bit more. Arcturians feel like they hold the galaxies on their shoulders, and Michael says that gets in their way sometimes. He says that sometimes *not* having that weight on *their* shoulders—like the Pleiadeans—gets in their way," I laughed. "They remind me of *don't worry 'bout a thing*," I began to sing (badly) about the Pleiadeans. "It's kind of Bob Marley-ish there on the Pleiades."

"Mmm," Douglas said.

"Oh! Because Bob Marley is Pleiadean," I said.

Maybe because I was beginning to lose the thread of the message as well as the sense of being in my current life, I was directed to focus on the soul-me that stood in front of me with her husband and three children.

"I can feel my children and my husband as if they're part of me. Their feelings and their thoughts, they're mine too," I said the tears running down my cheeks. "They're showing me this memory, so I can remember what it means to vibrate together, to lose the division," I sniffed. "And it's funny even though it's a memory, I can interact in the memory. You know I can talk to me which is so weird," I said. "I don't make many trips incarnated, not many at all. I don't have to anymore," I said.

"Incarnate?" Douglas asked.

"Yep."

"Yeah."

"Jamine visits this one often," I said referring to the life I was reliving. "It was a turning point."

I realized my place in this memory would soon come to an end, and nostalgia set in for a life and for people I hadn't even known existed thirty minutes earlier. My heart began to beat regret for not being able to stay. In Douglas's office, tears increased as I waited for the good-byes, and I took in every last breath of the experience.

"You visit this moment often in this life of mine. It is when you made the decision to accept this life," I said meaning Douglas' current human existence. "You're really young. In this life, you're really young; you're with another friend. Kind of in your 20s even though that doesn't make sense there. But if we were looking at it in earth time . . . .."

"Right," Douglas voiced his understanding.

"Kind of like in your 20s. Like that kind of brash *I'm-new-I've-gotta-good-job* kind of look going on. You're a hotshot in the Arcturian defenses," I told Douglas. "And we're teasing you about finding a wife," I said using *we* to incorporate the Pleiadean soul-me.

After a little while in the memory, it was hard to distinguish between the different soul parts of me. When I first stepped into the memory, I had a clear line between the then-me and the now-me, but as I became more and more comfortable, the line blurred.

"The souls of my children and my husband are with me in this life," I announced.

"Hmm," Douglas said; "in the same roles?"

"No. My dad was the husband in this life," I said blurring together my current and past lives. "That's the connection."

"I'm sorry; your dad in that life is your husband in this life?"

I shook my head *no*."

"No. The other way around."

"The other way around," I agreed.

"Your dad in this life was your husband in the other life."

"Yes, and he was . . ." I stopped as a realization dawned on me. "And my mother in this life was my daughter, and that sealed their soul contract together. My mom was an earth," I began and stopped. "She was a human having a physical experience on Pleiades, and she was so lost."

As I talked to Douglas, my parents from my current life stepped in with several examples of lives they had lived together. Although they met in a variety of roles—man and wife, father and daughter, brothers—theirs had always been a love story.

"There's almost a fire that's underneath the ground. Not geothermal," I said as I tried to make sense of what I was observing. "I don't know how to explain it, but you can see the sparks like sparklers," I said. "That's what it looks like. Like sparklers. You can see the sparks coming off the ground. Sparklers," I said again. And, then I panicked. "They're taking me away; I don't want to leave."

On the recording of the session, I could hear the sobs of my physical self as the archangels prepared me to leave the memory. I was unable to stand a reasonable argument for not going; it was, after all, a memory. The archangels allowed me to stay for a little while, taking in the surroundings, tuning into the vibration, reliving memories, touching the children and the husband of my past life, and reaching out to the soul-me for strength. I knew I would not see them again like this until I returned to soul. Then, I was told, I could visit these memories whenever I wanted.

"It's where we all made our decisions," I told Douglas.

"About this life?"

"It wasn't an easy decision," I responded. "The *me* there channeled too. Funny . . . she channeled Jasmine again. Jasmine said she's an old friend," I said and although I knew that Jasmine had made a joke, I was too heart-sick to acknowledge it as I said my good-byes. I was distraught. Like watching a loved one take a last breath, I was broken by good-bye. Michael radiated peace and Jasmine tried to restore the lightness to my soul. She joked until I laughed.

"Yeah. We all signed our contracts," I returned to the original discussion. "It's interesting. You don't usually sign your contracts in a physical life," I said authoritatively. "Well, I *guess* you don't," I said mockingly. "That's what they just told me," I explained. "But this was such a big thing. And really in earth time, it was 2000 years ago, but it moves so quickly."

"Mm-hmm," Douglas said as if he had known.

"This type of life is waiting for me in the next one. Jasmine knows. She's chosen it. Again, as a vacation," I laughed at the thought. "She's taking a physical existence kind of like a vacation," I reiterated. "My husband in that life signed his contract to come back as my father in this life," I said again.

"Wow!"

"So, he could guide me. So, he could make sure that I wasn't . . . that the joy in me didn't attract too much negativity. You signed your contract on the Pleiades," I told Douglas.

"Hmm."

"My husband said it had something to do with the beauty. You got lost in it and signed away, but it actually created a path for the rest of that life for you."

"Signing that contract?" Douglas asked.

"Yeah."

"Created a path in *that* life?"

"In that life," I responded.

"Interesting."

"You went on to do great things. So even though you had a bravado to you in your 20s which doesn't make sense for an Arcturian . . . but in earth years, around your 20s . . . you were really kind of shy," I giggled, "and lacked confidence in yourself, but having been asked to take this on—and we all knew; we saw would it would be—gave you confidence, made you risk, and you did great things," I told Douglas what I saw of his past life. "I'm hearing you were a colonel which, again, doesn't make sense for an Arcturian, but if you want to put it into something earth-related, it was colonel. This was also the life before you spent," I said and stopped. "This was also the life you stayed," I said and began to cry as I watched the choice that the soul-Douglas made in a past life.

Of all the things I've seen under hypnosis, the image of the Douglas-soul dying alone on the coal-black planet is the most upsetting. I have not yet fully described the scene I saw and felt and experienced, but I have seen it over and over again in nightmares and waking reminders of the crushing loneliness. Usually pretty adept at excising the ugly from my psyche, this one scene appears without warning. It is the darkness of the days and nights on the dead planet that is the most troubling aspect of the incredibly brave, but brutal end to the Douglas-soul. With nothing more than the equivalent of an iPhone light, the soul metered out his seven-day existence not by the setting of the sun or the rising of the moon, but by the intensity with which he questioned his choice. The later in the day it grew, the harsher he became about his decision. In the end, he begged for the small mercy of death as he succumbed to the virus that killed his comrade, the one who did not die alone, the one who died in his arms.

"To be honest, I'm actually really relieved that I'm standing in front of The Twelve and the archangels, you know," I said, not wanting to see any more of the death scene of the Douglas-soul. "It's lighter today," I said; "the archangels are playful, and the archangels watched me interact in my other life. I don't know how to explain the feeling," I began, "but there's a pang like . . . well . . . not heartbreak. They're always happy, but there's a wish, maybe that they could have experienced a physical life. Michael says that sometimes when you don't see the rain, you don't understand the sun. Right? I told him *sometimes too much rain is too much rain,*" I laughed. "There are two archangels who have had a human existence though," I relayed to Douglas.

"Metatron and Sandalphon," Douglas interjected.

"One is music," I said referring to the archangel's specialty. "One is music; one is children. I don't know what that means," I hesitated. "One specializes in the crystal children that are here."

"Mm-hmm," Douglas agreed.

"And Sandalphon is the beauty emanation. Music. Art. Beauty in the ideal; that's what it means," I said.

"Say that again?" Douglas asked.

"The beauty emanation is the ideal," I responded. Then, after a long pause, I added, "Yes, but the rest have not had human experiences."

"Right," Douglas agreed.

"Or physical experiences at all."

As I discussed the human incarnations of the two archangels, I felt myself searching for something I had read, and I dug through layer after layer of learning to understand why the two were given such a chance. No matter how hard I tried, however, I could not recall their stories. What I could remember, however, is that they are so tied to the earth realm—Sandalphon through the beauty and majesty of earth's physicality and Metatron through his connection to the legions of lightworkers or crystal children born on earth. Their incarnations, however, may be simply a misunderstanding. They may have been so visible in the dense physical space of earth that the visibility may have *implied* an incarnation.

"The Twelve can return to Source. They can merge back with Source," I told Douglas. "But they don't." I spent a long silence listening to their reasons; then added, "they choose physical manifestations much less than other souls. Far less often," I said. "But they do still, from time to time, take a human or physical form, and they're powerful enough that they can take many physical forms at one time."

"Mm-hmm," Douglas agreed.

"And they also sometimes step in for the very young and the very old who experience pain and give them relief," I said as I watched the many,

many scenes of their mercy. "Oh!" I exclaimed; "that's really beautiful. That's the mercy emanation."

"Hm."

"They'll step in and relieve the soul, so the soul has some respite, and then they'll accept the pain. There would be less pain in this world," I explained, "if there was more love, less division," I said as I felt Jasmine begin to take over.

My voice softened, but at the same time, became more confident, even, modulated. I no longer fought relinquishing control, and I was happy to explore other spirits and physical entities, new worlds and star systems and in between lives as Jasmine took control. Narrating rather than experiencing was tiring, and I missed so many of the interactions that happened simultaneously. Moreover, the hypnotic sessions had made the transition more normal, even natural. Jasmine made it easy; I had learned to trust her. And so, I just let go.

A Message from The Twelve: Love as the Amalgam of Many Vibrations

"This is the goal of the message," Jasmine said. "This world can choose whether it accepts the message or not. It can choose whether it accepts division or unity. But through this book, an emanation of joy will be broadcast. So, the words, themselves, will take the joy emanation. While the book is physical and flat, it will be touched by The Twelve. Simply by reading the words, the story will be affected, the story that humans live by, the story that humans created, the story that Astrals added to," she explained. "That will be affected simply by reading."

A long silence ensued as Jasmine spread the story out in front of me. Hundreds of thousands of years of story wherein humans learned to find their individuality in juxtaposition to another. We had honed this errant lesson to a brilliant, bewildering tangle of entitled individuality. The *us v. them* theme promoted a sense of power, but it missed the far greater power of unity, the far greater power of vibrating joy. Both at the collective level and at the individual level.

"And now you may ask questions," Jasmine told Douglas.

"Have we gotten the complete message?" he asked.

"No," Jasmine responded quickly.

"Okay."

"But you have the very core of the message. The heart of the message."

"So to speak," Douglas chimed in.

"He understood my joke," she whispered.

"I did. Can't be Arcturian all the time."

Although Jasmine responded, "you are not Arcturian now," Douglas's joke landed. She laughed at the stereotype of the Arcturians that Douglas had accepted, a stereotype that spotlighted one of the few weaknesses that came from an otherwise strength. In their zeal to protect, the Arcturians had forgotten how to let go and have fun.

"I'm not sure that's good or bad," Douglas laughed at her left-handed joke. "But yes."

"It's different."

"So it would seem."

"It would be easy for you to come to life again as an Arcturian, but now, you have stretched. You have taken on a lesson that was much harder, and you chose to for soul growth," Jasmine explained.

"Huh," Douglas said as he cued his next question. "I just figured I was on some Pleiadean drug or something," he joked.

"Just beauty. The beauty of the landscape. The vibration of joy," she said. "You lost your mind."

"Yeah. Apparently," Douglas said with sarcasm.

"You did find a Pleiadean wife on that trip," Jasmine teased. "It was a good life for you."

"I'm sorry," Douglas said; "I found a Pleiadean wife? Is that particular soul in my life today?"

"No. Not today. Not on your earth manifestation"

"Right," Douglas said. "So abstract to me."

"Ask the concrete questions."

"As I have gone through and heard these channelings, the stories, the information, the content, I have this feeling I'm missing something."

"Yes, you are," Jasmine assured him.

"Thank you. Of course, when you're missing something, it's very hard to ask for the thing that you're missing because you don't know exactly what it is that you're missing. It's a conundrum," Douglas explained.

"Mm," Jasmine agreed. "Have you noticed the pieces falling in place?"

"Well I was noticing the pieces *not* falling in place, to be honest with you," Douglas laughed. "Sixty-eight years old, and I'm having an existential crisis? That's a little old in this world," Douglas said.

"It's a good time."

"I'm sorry?"

"Like wine," Jasmine said.

"What's like wine?" Douglas asked.

"It's a good age."

"Sixty-eight?" Douglas asked, "to have an existential crisis?"

"Yes."

"Huh!"

"To wake you up," she said.

"Yeah. And as you're going to understand by the nature of the question, waking up to what?"

"To your true nature. To your real path," Jasmine answered. "To the contract you made with the group. To the ability to change, not just yourself, but a whole civilization."

"And am I resisting that?" Douglas asked the obvious.

"Of course."

"That's human," Douglas answered his next question.

"Yes," Jasmine answered, and I had the feeling of a crowd at a big sports stadium cheering for Douglas' breakthrough.

"Oh."

"And you shouldn't expect to be anything but human," Jasmine explained.

"Well . . . ."

"You are not Arcturian in this life."

"I understand that," Douglas said, "but I also understand that I'm supposed to be more than just this human *me*."

"Yes."

"So, when do you get that that's a conundrum from over here?" Douglas asked, giving the sense of usually placing himself *outside* the earth realm.

"Of course. Of course, but you chose this conundrum," she answered.

"Well we already know that I was under the influence," Douglas joked about his Pleiadean vacation.

Jasmine chuckled and then added, "But you had off-ramps in this life, and you know that. You recognize those life ramps. You could have chosen another mission."

"Huh. I didn't frame them that way because when you say it like that, nothing comes up. Like *oh, okay*."

"You journal. You take notes in your hard times," Jasmine said. "Look for your off-ramps," she said and, then, turned serious. "There is no wrong in failing in this mission. There is no wrong in choosing *not* to follow this mission, but there is all right in choosing it, and you know that at the soul level," Jasmine instructed.

"Yeah. I can't imagine not choosing it."

"That's because it's the soul you are."

"Okay."

"You've been apprenticed to that in your lives. That doesn't make sense to you, does it?"

"Kinda *yes* and kinda *no*," Douglas answered. "I mean it's like I structured lives to prepare for this?"

"Yes. Yes. And you had many more lives than she had," Jasmine said referring to me.

"Yes, so I've understood.

"You are battle-ready. You are battle-hardened for this choice," Jasmine explained.

"Mm-hmm," Douglas agreed.

"Not from this life alone, but from other lives. You know by instinct. Like muscle memory although it's not about muscle."

"It's a good thing . . . at sixty-eight," Douglas joked.

Both Jasmine and Douglas laughed. Douglas was clearly more comfortable interacting with Jasmine, and Jasmine was allowing him to explore his personality in their discussions.

"You have chosen well in your past lives. With a few exceptions."

Douglas laughed.

"No," Jasmine laughed. "I shall *not* tell you those," she said jokingly.

"I did my best," Douglas laughed. "Can we talk about being a warrior?"

"About being a lawyer?"

"A warrior. A warrior," Douglas repeated.

"A warrior. Yes."

"I've been thinking about that because, well, it would be like the Arcturians with the weapon."

"Yes."

"It's the same model essentially," Douglas explained setting up his question. "The warrior always has the weapon."

"No," she whispered.

"Well, I understood that," he laughed. "In our model. I think that's what I mean to say.

"Yes."

"There's always a warrior; he always has a weapon. Of course, he uses it very judiciously."

"No," Jasmine jumped in.

"No, I get that, so that's why I wanted to talk about your definition of warriors, how you're conceptualizing that."

"So, the weapons create a distance between you and the *other.*"

"Mm-hmm."

"Do you understand that?"

"I do."

"It is the vibration of joy here, of peace for an Arcturian, of humility, of beauty, of compassion and mercy. That is the tool you need, but in fear you choose a tool—a weapon—and not the tool that's at the soul level. And this makes sense on earth," Jasmine conceded; "your physical animal that houses your soul reacts in instinct. And when you are in this dense, physical body, you take on the attributes of the physical body: the instinct. And that instinct has created more division. It is not your fault—the human soul. It's not your fault; it was triggered by interference.

"In the DNA?"

"Yes. But while the trigger was from others, you have compounded it," she said. "A warrior is like the Archangel Michael; he does not kill."

"But he has a sword of light?" Douglas pointed out.

"Yes. It's light. It's just a metaphor for his vibration. This, just like the wings, are a metaphor for the angel. He doesn't really carry a sword. He's light," she explained. "He is a warrior."

As Jasmine discussed the sword of light as a metaphor, she was keenly aware that humans might not be able to accept the logic in the contrast. When she discussed the wings that are often displayed as part of the depiction of an angel, she explained that their light radiated so brightly with an almost-physical alive-ness that the fissures of light that spray from them can be interpreted by those having a physical experience as wings. Michael has been endowed with the Divine white light of love—the combined vibration of The Twelve and, more importantly, the emanation of Source. Its light stands out even in comparison to the gloriousness of his own light; often those in physical form see it as something separate: a sword.

"The image of him that you have on earth," Jasmine continued speaking of Michael, "of him standing on Satan's neck, shows you the power. Right? He has not killed or vanquished his enemy. He recognized himself in his enemy, and in so doing, he makes his enemy one with him. He unites. He brings them together."

"So, to stay with it then . . when we hand off fear to him, dark energy . . . ."

169

"To Michael?"

"Yes. He transforms it?" Douglas asked.

"Um . . . no."

"Well, what really happened? Douglas asked.

"He vibrates his light. He vibrates his emanation, and the darkness that you create as humans is powerless against it. It evaporates. Fsssh," Jasmine said mimicking the sound of evaporation. "It's like darkness and light when light is shone into a corner—a dark corner, the features of the dark corner become clear."

"Mm-hmm."

"Or when a child fears sleeping alone at night or fears what's in the closet or fears what's under the bed; the simple act of shining a light dissipates the fear. Michael's light dissipates the darkness that you talk about, but the creation of darkness is because of the division and hate on this planet," she explained. "But Michael is not the only one with light," Jasmine pressed.

"Oh no, I understood that," Douglas replied. "Just wanted a model to work with here. But darkness does not just exist on our planet?"

"No. It exists throughout the universes. It's a physical manifestation," Jasmine explained.

"Yes."

"It's part of free will," she announced. "The darkness in general doesn't begin in darkness. It begins with a viewpoint that's different, an alternative. An alternative that the physical being connects to so strongly that he begins the casting of the *other*. Do you see?" The kernel that creates the darkness is not done with the intent of creating darkness. It's done in separation. It's done in the separation of the *other*."

"And the dark wave that is coming toward the earth?" Douglas asked. "How does that fit in context with what you're saying?"

"The darkness is already here on earth," Jasmine responded. "Compounded. When the Astrals tried to manipulate the joy—the joy vibration—at first, they believed that they would help humans. Of course, they had an ulterior motive. Some thought it would be easier to carry out their mission."

"You mean the mining?" Douglas asked.

"No. The protection of the humans."

"Hmm," Douglas responded.

"That was their mission. The mining was secondary; that was free will. But as they manipulated, they lost control. Humans took to it; humans took to the change, and the divisiveness ran rampant. The darkness is here; the darkness has been here a long time," she explained.

"You had more you wanted to say."

"Go. You may ask."

"Then why are they talking about a dark wave coming to earth?" Douglas asked.

Jasmine chuckled, "The dark wave is here. The dark wave is here," she chuckled again. "There is nobody creating this anymore for humans. The humans compound it on their own."

"Then why is that model being used by spirit?" Douglas asked.

"No. No, not by spirit. No. No. No," she corrected him. "If you mean the vibrations that come that can cause, regrettably, issues in the environment or tragic deaths. The vibration is an energy impulse. It is meant for all good. It is meant to reinstitute joy, but the energy impulse is strong coming from the angels, coming from The Twelve, and therefore, there will be disruptions: tidal waves, earthquakes, volcanoes. It is regrettable, but if that's what you mean by the dark wave, that is . . .."

"So, I'm just going to paraphrase something I read and got. What I heard was that there is a dark energetic wave coming to earth, and if not enough lightworkers are awakened to who they are, it will envelop the earth."

"This is more of a metaphor for what you are experiencing now," Jasmine said. "And look if you look around the earth at this moment, you see that wave crashing in every single day."

"Yes."

171

"Yes. That is not through spirit. That is the creation. That is the story taking hold, being compounded. It is the division which creates the lack of unity which creates the lack of joy vibration. Each earth being can vibrate joy—individually—and it does have an effect. But the uniting of the planet in a joy vibration is so much more powerful and has so much more ability for change. So, the darkness that you talked about—the dark wave—is already here. The dark wave is a metaphor for the wave of division that is crashing over humans. You know that Astrals, too, are on a collision course. Their fate is tied now to the earth beings, and the Astrals have forgotten they're part of the Stellar group."

"I'm sorry," Douglas interrupted. "They have forgotten?"

"They're part of the Stellar group. They are Arcturians and Pleiadeans. There are others. If they can remember their foundation—their soul root—they could return."

"Mm-hmm," Douglas said, somewhat unsatisfied.

"You have more about the dark wave," she said.

"Well I'm trying to understand. You know, I'm trying to put all the pieces together, and I'm getting information from different sources, or it would seem different sources, and I think that's part of my confusion?"

"Singular source. We all emanate from Source," Jasmine said.

"Yes."

"All."

"So why do I feel I get all these different pieces that don't fit together?"

"They will fit together," Jasmine said. "But you're looking at them from the constraints of the human mind, so can you think about the last hypnotic session when she spoke about the Arcturians knowing? They knew the message was correct even though they stood tall against it. It's because they have to have time to integrate it within their framework right now," she explained. "Perhaps for you, maybe *story* is nebulous, and framework might be stronger in an understanding. Does that make better sense for you? A framework?"

"Yeah, probably. It doesn't feel so metaphorical."

"Yes. Framework then," she agreed. "So, the Astrals have a framework, a worldview that they imposed on the earth beings. You were too naïve and too underdeveloped at that point to know the difference and so they accepted it and expanded it into their framework. And now the framework is so strong that the division across the earth is *threatening* the earth, and the Astrals who helped create it. Both parties believe the framework so strongly that they can't see outside of it. Just as the Arcturians, their framework is they needed their weapon. Have you seen the weapon?" she asked and, then, answered: "you have."

"Okay. Apparently, I have."

"You know the power of it? It's devastating."

"Ah-hah," Douglas conceded.

"The Arcturians know at the soul level that is not their place to destroy creation. They know this, but they have created a framework of themselves, a story of themselves if you will, of protectors of the universe, and in a perverseness of that framework, they have created a weapon that they say will keep the peace by destroying part of creation. They know they are wrong, but it will take them some time to correct their framework. And depending on your framework, the pieces will fit better or not."

"And I assume that's just part of the agreement I made to work this through."

"Part of your problem in this life is that you know there is something bigger. You've always known that there's a bigger expansion that what you're capable of here, and that's one of the regrettable things of knowing you have another soul manifestation. You understand. You understand there's a different way of being. There's more knowledge than you can access in this existence, and it feels as if your intellect is in jail. Yes. As if your intellect is in jail."

"Mm-hmm," Douglas agreed.

"And you reach for the perfect understanding although you know—you *know* at the soul level—that you will not get it in this existence. You cannot," she told him.

"Mm-hmm," Douglas said a bit dejectedly.

"But when the messages are through—this first round of messages—it will begin to fit together. Puzzle pieces will drop into place. You don't have the full view yet."

"But you think I will be able to get that?"

"You will be able to get most of the view. You will still have questions, and you will still doubt. And that's part of being human."

"Well I feel that. Obviously as I'm putting this together, I need to subscribe to it."

"No," she answered. "No. Your job is to question it. This is your job."

"Even when the book is out?"

"Even when the book is out," Jasmine responded. "And within the book, you are to question. Remember she cannot see herself as she speaks. She has no sense of what it looks like. When she writes and listens to the tape, the recording, she is struck by the silence because she doesn't remember the silence. *You*," Jasmine said to Douglas, "are seeing it."

"Mm-hmm."

"This is part of your role: to ask the questions, to analyze what you see and what you've heard. That's why you have questions; it's part of your mission."

"Mm. And that's why you always ask me?"

"Yes. Your questions today are much more focused."

"Are they?" Douglas asked.

"Yes."

"And you make that as a fact of?"

"Confidence."

"Oh, heaven forbid," Douglas said sarcastically.

"Yes," she giggled. "it is part of your soul make-up to lack confidence."

"Is to lack confidence?" Douglas asked.

"Yes. It is a lesson you are learning, and you are learning it the hard way now."

"Even after all the lives I've lived?" Douglas asked.

"Yes."

"So my struggle with this isn't just at the human level?"

"Yes," she responded.

"It's at the very core?"

"Yes. You have the double soul, the double," Jasmine hesitated. "It is the need to deal with two competing frameworks and a message."

"You're talking about earth and Arcturian?" Douglas asked.

"Yes."

"It's not the same soul?"

"Same soul," she answered matter-of-factly. "You're living two frameworks now."

"Yeah. Okay. And this lack of confidence, that is at that soul level?

"Yes."

"Was that built in?" Douglas asked.

"No. It's your lesson. Some people have the inability to forgive. Some are awash in hubris. Others have other issues that they need to deal with in their life lessons. Yours is confidence," she said almost cheerfully. "But it is what makes you a great questioner. Do you see it's a gift as well?"

"The lack of confidence?"

"Yes."

"No, you're going to have to help me out with that one," Douglas laughed.

"It's your questioning. It's your lack of confidence that leads to your questions. Your questions lead to understanding and insight. If you were confident, you would not ask the questions. You would know. Do you see?"

"It's hard for me not to turn that into a negative trait," Douglas answered honestly.

"It is negative here on the earth," she responded. "It is a learning experience at the soul level, but every trait has its positive."

"And that was understood in context of the agreement?" Douglas asked.

"Yes."

"That's a complicated agreement," he joked.

"Yes," she laughed; "you saw the agreement even in a physical life."

"So, I had my chance to burn it, huh?" Douglas joked.

"Yes. Yes. You saw the agreement in a full form. You experienced it, you understood it, you had the emotions and feeling that you would have here, you saw some of the detractions and disabilities that you would have as a human, and you chose it anyway."

"It seems to me—from here—it's seems counter to being one of lack of confidence that would make that choice," Douglas stated his question.

"Because you look at it from the eyes of negative. It is a lesson that you need to learn, a lack of confidence. It's humility, you see. Right? A lack of humility, of truth in who you are, and it's a lesson that you need to learn. But it's not negative. It just is," she explained. "If you had more confidence you would not have found your path. You would have not noticed the feelings of something that you were supposed to do, the something that you knew was coming. You would have ignored it. Your lack of confidence helped you find your path."

"I think the argument that's going on is that I'm mixing up my higher self with my soul."

"Hmm. I think you do fine on that level. You have a lot of sources that is not available to most humans. Do you understand what I mean?"

"You mean because of my consciousness," Douglas asked for clarification.

"Yes."

"Yes. That is what confuses you. You've been told *there is no such thing*. People on the earth do not even see a great power, as if everything just happens."

"Mm-hmm."

"It's obvious," she laughed; "it's obvious. And so you are distracted by what *should* be at the earth level—what you're *told* should be—and what you know, what you experience as a soul. But for the most part, you follow your guidance well, and I think you know that."

"I try to." Douglas said.

"Yes."

"It's moments like the last week where I don't feel like I'm following any guidance because I'm in such a swirl," Douglas said. But I think that must be that function of reconfiguring."

"Framework," Jasmine whispered.

"Framework. Right," Douglas agreed. "I think in a sense almost expanding it."

"Yes. Expanding and deleting some of the pieces that don't serve you."

"Mm. Okay. I'm working on the deletion part. I'm not sure I'm doing too well."

"It will happen. There is no time in which you have to solve this puzzle. You are not on a timer," Jasmine assured Douglas.

"The book can be written. I can write what I have to write without it being solved?" Douglas asked.

"Yes. In fact, the act of writing will help you solve some of those pieces."

"Hmm."

"It is time for her to return," Jasmine referred to me.

"Okay. Thank you for coming and chatting with me."

"Have you felt the archangel Gabriel around you lately?" Jasmine asked.

"If I have, I've not identified it in that way," Douglas responded.

"Feel for him. Or her. You see Gabriel as a female?" Jasmine asked. "Yes?"

"Yeah, I think I do."

"Okay. Feel for *her*. She will help you write. That's part of your angst."

"Hmm. Okay."

"She is the communicator, and you won't be perfect. You know this, yes?"

"Um yes and no," Douglas chuckled.

"Your words will spill on the page the best that they can be; just allow Gabriel to guide you. You will not guide yourself. If you try, you will try to be perfect and nothing will come out on the paper. But allow Gabriel to guide you, and it will happen."

"Okay."

"And once you start, you'll feel his presence. Her presence."

"Mm-hmm." After a long silence, Douglas added, "okay. Thank you and thank you for encouraging me with the questions."

As Jasmine disengaged from the part of the soul that is me, I experienced the pang of leaving her and our shared memory from our life in the Pleiades. Unlike the way *to* my sacred space, the way back to the physical realm moves much more quickly. As I move through the process, layers of light shower me, cleansing me, preparing me to reengage in the denser, constraint-driven setting. The archangels—all of them—circle around me and re-tune my vibratory calibration; the longer I am with The Twelve, the stronger my vibration becomes. Such a high vibration would call attention to me on the earth plane and would adversely affect me and my ability to transmit the message.

Just before I exit my sacred space, a final shower of Divine white light moves in through the crown on the top of my head, enlightens every single building block of my physical body, and exits out through fingertips and toes, eyes and mouth and ears. I stand a spectacle of light and love, and I radiate it out through the universes.

This time, when I reemerge into my body and through my sacred door back to my current existence, I am given a glimpse of alternative paths, paths that a successful mission would make possible. It is the first time I see an alternative; it is the first time I reemerge with, on balance, hope.

ACT VI

The Immensity and Almost-Eternity of Souls

2 July 2019

We all shine on . . . like the moon and the stars and the sun . . . we all shine on . . . come on and on and on.

John Lennon

Understanding the Place of the Soul in the Universes

They collected souls as they collected jewels.
~John Steinbeck

In the week leading up to the sixth session, I bumped into poets and sages who had long understood the message that would save us. One, a long-haired, hippie-type, sang it out for all of us to hear. "All you need is love," he said simply. After six hypnotic sessions in which love was shown to be the rainbow-white amalgamation of all positive vibrations in the universes, I began to think he was on to something. Our natural human state, I have come to learn, is to link together in joy. While I have been lucky enough to hear this through the insistent thoughts of ascended beings, I have also recognized the intuitive logic that lays at the heart of the message. It is obvious what brings us joy. It is association with others. The simple act of another's hand touching ours drives happiness, contentment, sometimes even bliss. Think of the finger-wrap of a baby's tiny grip or the shy, butterfly-light grasp of first love or the age-steadying embrace of older parents. These are the harbingers of joy, and we experience it regularly simply by touching another's hand. If we parlayed that touch to the soul level, the experience would be overwhelming, mind-blowing.

When I think back on all the profound moments of my life, I realize they were all about simple human interaction. They did not translate well to writing because they were so ordinary, so every day. Yet, many of them resonated deeply at the soul level, so when I think of them now, I am transported to the very moment of the memory. Just like the memories I experience—fully experience—when I am in the spirit world.

When I was newly graduated with a doctorate in education, I was invited to keynote a professional conference. It was my first big professional gig. As the mother of a child under one, I didn't know how to juggle motherhood and professor-hood. Before I turned down the invitation, however, I asked the two people I trusted most in the world for help: my parents. Their response was the obvious one. "We'll go with you," they said. And we were off to Pittsburgh with an almost newborn and a car full of baby supplies. The only thing that marked the trip as anything professional was the laptop tucked away between the carriage and the playpen.

As I set up the computer and screen for my speech, my father tagged along to help. "Can I watch you present?" he asked. Normally in control and with an acerbic wit, my father seemed shy in the academic arena. Brilliant but unable to attend college, my father was book smart, not classroom smart, and it showed in his lack of confidence at the conference. From the back of the room, he watched me present, unwilling to take a chair from one of the conference attendees. When I cracked a joke, he laughed and nodded his appreciation; I smiled when he gave me a *thumbs up* sign halfway through, and although an audience sat in front of me, I spoke to an audience of one. He, I could tell, was impressed.

Close to the end of the presentation when the overly basic PowerPoint was winding down in the semi-lit room and the audience members were asking questions, I looked back to see my father crying. And I mean crying. Hankie out, my father dabbed at the water pouring from his eyes. When he blew his nose, the audience turned to him. Embarrassed, he blurted out in a cracked voice, "That's my daughter," and he pointed to me in the front. The audience turned to see me tear up and, then, they burst into applause. As they left the room, they commented on my father's pride more often than on what I had actually said, but my heart swelled with love as I lived the connection between my dad and me. And I know if I looked back through my life, there would be many, many such moments of profound connection and deep joy. I know it because it is our natural state.

Our joy, combined with the vibrations of so many other physical beings throughout the universes, converts to Divine white light; it converts to love. It is, I have learned over these last few sessions, the highest, most sacred emotion. Yet, for too long, we have allowed division to deaden that most Divine-inspired sensation; we have allowed our separation, our individuality to reign supreme in a world where connection makes more sense. When we come together, we simply *feel* better. When we come together, we understand who we are at the soul level. We remember our mission. We reconnect with the joy vibration in our souls. And we recognize the simple truth in the laughter that marks our connections; laughter is the canary in the coal mine that predicts joy. This is the message.

The Sixth Hypnotic Session:
The Soul's Magnitude of Knowingness

"You're at that door to your sacred space. Open it. Step through and close the door behind you. And just fill me in when you're ready," Douglas said to mark the end of the hypnotic count.

When I first step through into my sacred space, there are always a few minutes of silence as I adjust to the new reality. There is clarity, a deep understanding of concepts and issues and the proverbial meaning of life that swirls around me waiting for my opened senses to accept. Here on earth, we are satisfied with five senses—sight, touch, smell, taste, and sound; however, there are more when we are ready to accept them. An intuitive sense, for example, with which we understand by just knowing, and a harmonic sense in which the essence of beings around us becomes sharper, more known by the sound of the energy around them.

So, when I first arrive in my sacred space, I allow the extra senses to encircle and envelope me as I adjust to them. Since they are carried by Divine White Light, it is not unpleasant; instead, it feels like a whirlpool opening of expanded consciousness. It reminds me a little of the closing scene of the old 1960s *Get Smart* TV show where, as the actor walks through, all the screen doors and iron gates and heavy entrances slam shut, impenetrable and menacing-like. Except in reverse. In the spirit world, every barrier is blown open. Every door is undone, and access is granted to everything.

"I don't want to start because I know when I do, it will change," I told Douglas.

"What will change?" Douglas asked, an uncharacteristically early question.

"This," I said gesturing to the myriad spirit beings in front of me. "This welcoming."

"Mm," Douglas replied.

"I'm afraid when I acknowledge the welcoming, it will change. It won't be a welcome anymore."

"Hmm," Douglas said in a way that asked for more detail.

As I stood on the landing just outside the door from the earth realm, I looked at the souls of loved ones—some who I knew in my present earth life, some from other lives. Their glow welcomed me into the space. A joy permeated the very large crowd, and their spirit touches activated memories of the past from both my current incarnation and past ones. Regardless of the life, however, I recognized each and every memory. I was not confused by the random nature of the memories; I understood that they were based on whichever soul had brushed by me last. I wasn't upset by the out-of-my-current life memories either. I just accepted them; I filed them away as I would any other memory.

"I'll already be welcomed, Archangel Michael said," and then changed gears. "My father and mother guided me up the steps. Michael was behind us. My mom is very shy in spirit; she's just getting her footing," I explained. "My dad is *not* shy," I added. "He told me all kinds of things."

I had a long conversation with my parents, one that took many hours to complete, but lasted only seconds in earth time. My dad began the conversation by gesturing to the silky white, flowing pants I was wearing.

Lose the pants, he said, suggesting in his comment that they were odd-looking.

Really? I snarked back; *actually, I like them,* I said drawing them out from my hips with both hands.

All this took place in spiritual space, of course, but it was so reminiscent of an earth interaction with my father that I knew it was him. It was the word play between us that warmed me. It just felt right.

"On the top of the steps," I stopped and giggled, "my whole big Irish family was there. Some that I didn't even . . . ," I stopped. "I know better than to say this, but I'm going to say it anyway . . . even some I didn't like," I said referring to the spirit family that greeted me. "But they had a different feeling," I explained

"Mm-hmm," Douglas gestured his understanding.

"And there were some who are still in physical form here on the earth, but the part of their soul that's here was there to greet me too."

Although my response was matter-of-fact, I knew at the human level this was something big, something I would need to explain. Yet in the moment, I completely understood the splitting of souls into parts for incarnations. In fact, I acknowledged the presence on the spirit side of my daughter and son and our little dog, all of whom are still safely within the confines of the physical reality of earth.

Our souls are immense. While there are boundaries, the boundaries appear at the very edge of infinity. The reach and scope of a soul's understanding also bumps right up against infinity, so there is no way such an immense energy could inhabit a physical being. Instead, a little bit of the soul is cleaved to be part of a physical existence, an existence contracted by our full soul in the spirit world. Depending on the size of the piece of soul, we might more easily maintain contact with the spirit world or get flashes of past existences. Artists of all stripes have souls that are big enough to remember the ideal, and they paint or sing or write or in some way bring the ideal to life in the physical space of earth.

Too much soul is dangerous, especially in an earth existence where sensations are so dense. We *feel* sensations so fully, so acutely. Sometimes these sensations are *physical*: for example, the first time we hold a child in our arms, the pain of a lost love, the exhilaration that comes with a hard-fought triumph. We are slowed by these sensations; we allow sensations to guide our thoughts and actions rather than relying on intellect as a guide, and they often knock us off the path to completing our missions.

Sensations are also the reason the archangels envy us; well . . . not *envy*. That's not the right word. But there is a little pang of the no-sensation the archangels recognize when they're with humans. It is the reason why, when Jasmine speaks through me, she delights in the sensations she feels. As she speaks with Douglas, Jasmine also travels the earth. She chooses to explore through the sense organs of my physical body. The last stand of a blood moon just before it gives way to the glorious sunrise and the aurora borealis-like colors of the sunsets that deepen gradually into the soft black and twinkling light of the night sky, the green-green of the jungle swelter and the vast emptiness of the desert tans, the wrinkled warmth of the mighty elephant and the gentle spill of water from the cup of the calla lily are so much more pleasurable through the sense organs of the human body. The experience of such sensations is overwhelming for a physical body with a soul that has the capacity for endlessness; so, most of our soul resides in spirit to protect the incarnation.

"My Aunt Catherine opened the door to my sacred place," I told Douglas; "I gave her *the look*, but she did it on purpose. It was mischievous," I laughed. "I wanted her to close it, so I could open it," I explained; I wanted to follow Douglas' commands. "But they wouldn't. And, then as I walked through, I was afraid they wouldn't follow me, but they were already in front of me," I explained. "Silly me. I expected them to walk through the door."

As I described the scene on the stairs to Douglas, I continued to greet the souls that surrounded me. Without the bother of physically producing words, I was able to have personal conversations with many of them at the same time. All I had to do was touch and be touched. I was unencumbered by the physical necessity of forming words; instead, thoughts were exchanged immediately, and a download of sorts sat ready for discovery at a later, more convenient time for me.

"The archangels are in a ring in front of me and in front of the crowd of my family," I continued to describe the scene. "I asked for my family," I said; "well, I asked for my parents, but they're all here. And the archangels are in a semi-circle—like a ring—in front of the group. All of them," I said referring to the archangels. "And The Twelve are already here. I'm becoming stronger. I can just can meld with them right away," I explained to Douglas.

For a few seconds, I stopped to listen to the directions of The Twelve. Although I have generally understood immediately what is expected of me, it often took me some time to figure out how to explain it in English. This was one of those moments.

"They want me to clarify Jasmine," I announced to Douglas. "I write about her as if she's singular, but she's a manifestation of all of them," I said referring to The Twelve.

"Ok, okay," Douglas replied.

"It's just that they put my soul piece in the *they*," I tried to explain, "in the voice of *they* so that I have an easier time merging and, then, giving up control," I said.

What I was trying to articulate was the fact that the greater part of my soul—the soul part that remained in the spirit world—resided in what I called *Jasmine*. When I travel to the spirit world in a hypnotic state, I merge with the greater part of my soul—Jasmine. In doing so, there is a natural give-and-take between the soul-me and my greater soul. It is comfortable, natural, my soul's normal state. The Twelve choose to speak as one through Jasmine because it is easier for me to relinquish control of my mind and ego to an entity that represents the greater me. While I call the part of The Twelve that speaks *Jasmine*, all of The Twelve participate in speaking through me.

"It's okay if I call her *she*. It's okay if I talk about her as Jasmine, but it's *they*. And others can speak through Jasmine as well," I said. "Others can add their own voice. Higher beings. Ascended," I said to narrow down the *others* of my previous statement.

There was a significant silence as I began to understand my role for the day. As I was being given instructions, not like on earth, but in a multimodal way, I was told to describe what I was seeing. It would fill the void while I absorbed the intent of The Twelve.

"There's a movement to the atmosphere," I began. "We're in spirit space; we're not physical," I told Douglas.

"Okay."

"You know those old movies where they show ghosts or spirit in just a white sheet? Like a humanoid shape of white? Kind of veil-like? Just moving around in the space, in the physical space?" I asked. "They do that because they remember it from the life in between. There's a movement of souls," I said. "It's nice," I admitted. "If you have a white sheer scarf, and you feel it brush against you in a breeze, it's pleasant," I said working to explain the feeling of spirit touch.

My language became slow and deliberate as I explained the movement of souls in the atmosphere. I wanted to feel, not narrate. In the spirit world, I could see myself standing, eyes closed, back arched, arms outstretched as spirit moved past me and through me and around me. My hair blew in the breeze their movement created. My face shone serene.

"And there are souls coming today to watch," I announced. "And as they come through, I can feel their brush against me. It's not just a physical feeling—a physical sensation of them touching me," I said, "but there are histories and emotions and feelings and connections that are kind of like instantly conveyed to me. Their touch . . . it's so pleasant," I reiterated.

When my children were young, we would give each other *butterfly kisses*. Eyelashes would flutter against cheek to create a sensation of barely touching. It tickled, but not really. It was a mere hint of contact. A sweet caress. Spirit touch is like a butterfly kiss. But because there are innumerable souls that brush past, the sensation is compounded exponentially, a myriad of lovely almost touches.

189

"There's a music that just," I said and stopped to consider how to articulate the thought. "Umm *infiltrates* is a negative word, but ... like every cell in my body is soaking the music as I walk."

"How about *permeate*?" Douglas asked

"Permeate," I agreed. "And it's meant to attune me. Something big is coming today," I announced and, then, returned to the discussion of music. "When I was a little girl ... I know I talked about this earlier ... when I was a little girl, there was an amusement park that had a swimming pool, and they piped music in through the pool. The speakers were under the water, and when you dove into the water, you could hear this distorted music. And it was really cool, and that's how it feels," I explained.

As I go through this experience, I'm struck by how often I recognized the spirit world in my earth incarnation, and if I'm to be honest, it was more clear to me when I was younger than when I allowed the expectations of what *should* or *should not be* get in my way as an adult. I've written and spoken about the music piped into the pool at Knoebel's Grove Amusement Park many times over the years; there was just something about it that haunted me. I recognized a memory, a foundational sense of *what is* at the soul level. The piped-in music at the pool came up in my life over and over again because I recognized it though I could not name it. Throughout my life, there were so many seemingly simple, simply unremarkable "really cool" things that bubbled up such strong emotions in me. Just like the music piped through the water at Knoebel's Grove Amusement Park's pool.

"It's not in the water; it's in the air," I said referring to the music of the spirit world. I mean, there's not really air, but it's just everywhere. And when you turn, the music changes, or when you're touched by another being, the music changes. I don't even think music is the right word," I said. "I keep hearing the word *harmonics*. It's harmonics, and sometimes the soul's name is a harmonic, not words or letters, and sometimes a soul's name is a feel, a touch."

It is impossible to name the souls with names that are formed from a harmonic or a feel, but it is possible to honor and acknowledge their existence. When I stood among them, we were linked. Reunited, really. And I recognized their essence in the names they chose.

"It's a formal gathering, but it doesn't happen often," I said about the gathering souls. "And the souls from different soul groups meet souls from the other soul groups, and so there's a sense of like a picnic in the park. A community picnic," I explained the feeling of the gathering. "And everything is showered by The Twelve vibrating together. The Divine white light," I explained. "It's physical. You can see it everywhere. You can feel it," I said. "What I see is crystalline structure inside the white, and when it comes in contact with the soul's light, it sparkles a different color. It's not the right thing to say that a soul has a color based on its rank, but the soul has a color based on its rank," I said anyway. "It's in the process of learning and ascending, and the color isn't for other people. It's for the soul, itself, to remember. So, in that sense, it's not hierarchical at all; it's like having a diploma. It's a celebration. Almost like how military officers wear their rank, but not hierarchical. It's recognizing success," I explained.

Soul color distinguishes levels of learning. Although The Twelve radiate a deep purple color that marks them as ascended, they are not considered any better than the soul that radiates a light golden yellow. These souls are the novices. They are relatively new. Yet, their pale, sparkling yellow connotes as sense of accomplishment that is just as acknowledged as the deep purple of the ascended.

"When The Twelve are together, and they radiate, it's like a display around them," I described their essence to Douglas. "It's the light that's so bright that it can't be contained, and there's like a buzz—an electrical field—that's moving in and through everything right now," I said. Then, I changed directions to inform Douglas that "Jasmine has called me to her. She doesn't have a hand," I explained, but she put out what looks like, to me, a hand to come to her."

"Mm-hmm," Douglas agreed.

A long silence ensued as I merged with The Twelve. My soul piece took its place within the larger soul that I called Jasmine. That larger soul was cosmically expanded by merging with the rest of The Twelve. *As above, so below,* I heard over and over again, and I understood that the universe works on connection, union, *not* division. We all—every single soul—emanate from Source. We are holograms of each other, part of a unified whole. We choose to cleave our souls into pieces to extend the learning that we need to ascend to the point where we can reintegrate, once again, with Source. It is a process through which we build the vibration of love by unity, a vibration that resonates throughout the universes and into infinity. I cannot wholly understand *why* this is the process, but I intuit a need, a drive, a desire to do it.

"I've come back to *them,*" I gasped. "What I can see is amazing. It's magnificent. I can see stars being born, and I can see stars dying," I began to narrate. "And the creation of galaxies and universes. I feel the power of stepping into a black hole," I said. "And it's just regular," I marveled.

The soul group of The Twelve that I had been allowed to experience was so expansive, so limitless, so unrestrained that together they experienced the building and breaking apart of planets and star systems and universes as a regular part of their existence. While mind-bending and almost mind-numbing to someone in a physical existence like me, to them, it simply was.

"I have this feeling of expansion," I tried to explain; "things breaking apart and building and always, always, always expanding," I said. "I can go to the records," I told Douglas, referring to the Akashic Records, "and I know everything. I'm not allowed to say what I know there," I admitted. "And I can feel the energy of Source," I said in awe. "And there," I said referring to Source, "I feel contracting too. And things I don't know. And things I can't explain. And things I have no words for. And this is normal for The Twelve. It's just like their peripheral vision," I said as a way to illustrate the typical and ordinary in the extraordinary. "It's just normal for them. And if you can imagine that these Ascended Masters have a core or a heart," I said. "they feel the beating of *every single soul* no matter where they are," I said drawing out and emphasizing each word. "They know. They know each soul. I can feel the beating of whole ... whole planets, and in the beating of a whole planet, I can feel *all* of the individual souls beating as one. It's collective," I said. "But it's individual too, and I can feel when one soul moves out of the collective. It's like a master control panel of all the souls, and you can feel those that are disconnected," I said.

As I found and focused on the earth realm in my tour of what The Twelve experienced as normal, I was saddened by the dispossessed, those who felt their singularity so keenly. Their souls resonated with their natural instinct to connect, yet they found themselves alone without hope. It was not a matter of poverty; in fact, although there were many souls drowning in their inability to provide for the basic wants of a physical incarnation, there were just as many who had more than enough. Too much actually. The feeling of singularity wasn't a matter of gender or geographic area, intellectual ability, professional success, or birth order. Rather, these souls had not figured out how to protect themselves from the crushing loneliness that the division in our race demanded. They were utterly, hopelessly, aimlessly alone, unconnected.

"And you can feel the tension in our universe of all the souls wondering *what will happen to earth*? And if it happens, one second we're here and one second we're not. It vaporizes, but there's an energy impulse that just *ripples*," I emphasized the result of the earth ending; "ripples across the universes. Powerful most in our own universe," I explained; "enough to set back whole civilizations. Like a winter. Metaphorically like a winter. That's why the Stellars are so concerned," I said.

I understood, as I had not understood before, how the end of humanity could affect the rest of the universes. I had been shown over and over again how our souls are pieces of the whole, how are souls are holograms of each other emanating from Source. And although as we live in physical incarnations, we are different from each other—humans and Pleiadeans and Arcturians, Stellars and Astrals—we are all the same at our essence. We all beat to and from the same Source. So, when something happens to one of us, there is a ripple effect for all of us. At the individual level. And at the universe level.

"They can lose so much of their growth," I explained. "Like when the waters ravaged the earth here, and so much was lost," I said although I only had a vague understanding about what I was trying to explain. "Huh! We haven't yet caught up to the ancient Egyptians," I said, slowly enlarging my understanding, "Or the Andalusians or the Mayans," I added. "And it could have the same impact on the universe. They're better prepared, the Stellars are," I assured Douglas. "They catalogued their history. They've made reparations . . . no, not the right word," I stalled. "They've made *preparations* for what might happen," I said as I was given a front-row seat to one possible, apocalyptic scenario. "Their recovery will be different from what the earth experience 11,000 years ago," I said referring back to the waters that ravaged the earth. "But it will still be generations to recover."

I was shown a time when humans were more advanced intellectually, spiritually, and technology-wise than we are now. There was a devastating flood—like the epic kind that resides in the story of Noah. Ice caps shifted. The climate chilled. The landscape changed, and human progress was not only delayed but set back centuries. We have not yet recovered, I was told while I was in the spirit world.

"The Arcturians stood ready to vaporize the earth before we vaporized ourselves, but they stood down," I said. "They know whether we do it, or whether they do it, the effect will be the same. Or close enough," I corrected myself. "And the Arcturians also understand now that what might look like an inevitable could also change, so they're less—not all of them—they're less desirous of pulling the trigger," I told Douglas. "The earth was created with such joy," I said with a tinge of sadness. "Even the physical features were meant to bring joy," I said wistfully. "And what an experiment to have so many different features: the desert, the ocean, the mountains. Each ecosystem brings joy in a different way and allows humans to move from one to the other to remember: if you live in the woods your whole life, you take the woods for granted," I explained. "When you see the desert, you remember that the woods are beautiful."

A long silence ensued as Jasmine took me across the earth to witness, on my own, the beauty, the pure joy of the earth landscape. Although it happened quickly in earth time, Jasmine took her time on the spirit side to allow me to experience it with all my senses. I smelled the heat of the desert and the rain of the Indian monsoon. I touched flowers with tiny shards of glass-like leaves and felt the warmth of sand between my toes as I walked the beach of a blue-green sea. I heard the whine of hyenas and the roar of lions, the cries of newborns and the sound of whales slapping back into water. Although I had always loved to travel and explore, to see it all in one simultaneous, multi-sensational sprint across the earth was magnificent. Playing out in tandem to such beauty, however, was the division of the population that inhabited the magnificent place.

"My heart is heavy," I cried. "In the network of individual souls, I can hear the anger of individual souls," I said. "For such stupid things," I added.

When Jasmine noted my sensitivity to the sounds of anger, she returned me to the spirit world. Together, we celebrated the beautiful, daily miracles that function as reminders of the natural state of human beings. I saw the faces of newborns and the smile of a grateful older parent. We saw the light break through the clouds on an otherwise grey day and reveled in the sleek, illuminating ray of that spark on the earth. We saw the wagging tail of the accepting dog and the purr of the arched-back cat rubbing against legs. The sun on a face, the glint and twinkle of light on water, the light breeze of an early fall, the colors of leaves and flowers and people. All reminders of joy. If only we noticed them. If only we lived by them. If only we remembered the power of connecting with each other.

"They're showing me the moment my mother held me the first time, and the absolute joy and connection that we had. That connection is what we lost," I said meaning humans, not my mother and me. "We experience it from time to time on the individual level, but that connection can be replicated. Across the planet. All the time. Every day," I said.

A Message from The Twelve: Reintegrate the Other for Wholeness

A long silence marked the transition between my descriptions and Jasmine's. I had no difficulty relinquishing control because I had already fully merged with Jasmine, and through her, with The Twelve. The much more powerful and prescient part of my soul simply stepped in.

"And now you can ask questions," she directed Douglas. "She won't have long," Jasmine warned Douglas about me.

What she meant is that being part of such an expansive soul group would slowly eat away at my ability—or, rather, *their* ability—to extricate my little bit of soul from the whole. The more comfortable I became, the less the soul-me stood out, distinct from the rest. I would also be less willing to return to the dense physical existence despite the love I held for my family and friends and the beauty of the earth.

"Okay," Douglas agreed. "I'm trying to truly capture this concept—the full concept—of the definition of Stellars and Astrals. Let's start with Stellars; I think I got it," he said. "I'm assuming Stellars refer to any incarnated intergalactic being that's part of the Federation," Douglas said, referring to the loose connection of like-minded, higher-dimension star dwellers.

"Or outside the Federation as well," Jasmine corrected him.

"Oh both," Douglas said.

"Mm-hmm," Jasmine agreed.

"So, is it any incarnated being other than humans?"

"Yes."

"Okay," Douglas singled his understanding. "Just want to make sure I got that right."

"And Astrals are Stellars," Jasmine affirmed.

"And yet they're not," Douglas countered.

"And yet they're not."

"And I don't get it because you're telling me the souls are identical," Douglas said.

"Mm-hmm."

"So, the souls have no contamination," Douglas stated.

"Mm-hmm."

"So then . . . ."

"They contaminate on earth," Jasmine interjected. "In a physical existence."

"So that's by soul agreement?" Douglas asked.

"The Astrals' soul agreements are different," she answered. "They come with the idea to protect. With the idea to spread peace. Whatever their soul contract—the collective contract is—and yet because of where they land, they are contaminated, right?" Jasmine asked Douglas. "Because of who they are in contact with in the physical realm, they can be corrupted in the physical realm," Jasmine said. "Think of it as a child who was born to a family that projects kindness and goodness and shelters the child in kindness and goodness. The child grows in kindness and goodness. The child has the basis for being a kind and good human," she explained. "Think of a child who is born to a family that does not radiate the same or who radiates the opposite. The child's soul is as pure in the beginning as the child whose parents or family radiate kindness and goodness, but the child learns in the physical body that kindness and goodness is for the weak. It's the same with the Astrals. They're born pure souls," Jasmine stated, "but it's the physical destination, the physical connections they make that determine whether or not they fall in line. Not all Astrals end up believing the story. Or some may believe the story for some time, but then leave the story. But they are *not* welcomed back by the Stellars," she said.

As Jasmine talked of the Astrals being unwelcomed by the Stellars, I couldn't help but think of the character in Harper Lee's classic, *To Kill a Mockingbird*. Mayella Ewell, the hapless daughter of the drunk, vulgarian, resident of the town dump. The home of Bob Ewell was described as "the playhouse of an insane child" with remnants from the dump repurposed to serve as an aesthetically-void home for the family, including Mayella. In the novel, we get a glimpse of Mayella's personality when Lee writes:

> Against the fence, in a line, were six chipped-enamel slop
> jars holding brilliant red geraniums, cared for as tenderly as
> if they belonged to Miss Maudie Atkinson . . . . People said
> they were Mayella Ewell's.

Like the Astrals, however, Mayella suffered from the onus of her family name and background. *Once contaminated*, the town's people thought, *always contaminated*, and Mayella's lot was cast with her father's despite the obvious contradictions. For all their enlightened ways, then, the Stellars had painted all Astrals with the same brush stroke; *once an Astral*, they maintained, *always an Astral*.

"Because?" Douglas asked in a slow rise.

"Because the Stellars have casted them," Jasmine said referring to the Astrals, "as the *others*. But the humans have accepted the Astrals that have broken free of the story, and in this way, humans who are not as advanced as the Stellars, end up being more advanced in their acceptance."

"What drives that acceptance?" Douglas asked.

"I'm sorry?"

"I'm trying to understand why the humans have this capacity?"

"Because humans on an individual level vibrate joy," Jasmine chuckled, "and so individually they are much more accepting, much more trustworthy, much more trust*ing*," she said. "They accept."

"Because they believe in redemption?"

"Hm. I don't think that's at the soul level. Some do," she said. "I think it's purely because if you can radiate joy, you radiate joy, and acceptance is part of that joy radiation."

"Hm. Okay," Douglas said.

"And humans are funny in that they may cast a whole group as the *other*, and yet accept and love individuals from the group they hate. The Stellars have advanced beyond that contradiction, and yet, in advancing beyond that contradiction, they have regressed," Jasmine explained. "It is a good thing that humans can accept at the individual level. The goal is to get them to accept at the group level. At the collective. At the planet-wide level," Jasmine said.

"Why do . . . why are . . . I'm changing subjects," Douglas announced. "I got that piece as much as I can in this moment," Douglas laughed.

"You are human," Jasmine joked.

"So, I'm learning; then I say *What? I thought I had this down*," Douglas joked. "Because . . . yeah . . . it has to do with the soul level versus incarnated level . . .".

"Yes!"

"And getting them essentially mixed up."

"Yes! Yes, this is a big step for you," Jasmine said with congratulations.

"I'm trying," Douglas laughed.

"And notice the confidence that you had to use to say that," Jasmine pointed out.

"You noted some of that?

"I did."

"Thanks," Douglas said.

"And I congratulate you."

"Thanks."

"And I honor you."

"Oh! Well thank you. Will you write that down and date it?" Douglas joked while Jasmine laughed.

"Well, as you know better than I, I'm sure I had to make a decision to quit feeling sorry for myself and to move forward, and your encouragement to write, of course, was very helpful. And as you know, that has begun."

"And it expresses your inner-most feelings."

"Yeah. They're there, huh?"

"Yes."

"Well that's good," Douglas said, "because it feels so cludgie."

"We will guide you," Jasmine assured Douglas in a calm voice.

"Thank goodness. I'm assuming there will be a whole process with you after the chapters have been channeled. After we sort through things and get clarity and etcetera, etcetera."

"Yes. She will not like to hear this," Jasmine began referring to me, "but there's one more session where the message comes through for the part of the message that you will have, and then after that, a session for formatting. It will be shorter; it will not be as hard on her. But she will have to do it."

"Okay."

"We do not want to mix up the message with the way the message is presented."

"Hm. Okay."

"She likes the stars," Jasmine announced to Douglas, seemingly unconnected to the greater conversation.

"And for good reason."

"She likes to touch them. She is amazed by this."

"She's not coming back, huh?" Douglas joked.

"Oh she will," Jasmine asserted.

"Yeah. I got that," Douglas laughed. "Despite herself."

Douglas did not know how close his joke was to right. Jasmine drew my attention to my thoughts in the moment of her announcement about the stars. While there are no actual hands in the spirit world, I will sometimes have the sensation of using my hand or being touched by a hand. In the case of the stars, my phantom physical hand could reach out and touch them. For me, it gave me the sense of the enormity of a soul and the infinitely larger enormity of being linked to The Twelve. My hand was roughly the same size as the star. My spirit hand, in other words, could almost, but not quite, hold a star in it. The physical size of the sun—the earth's star—has a diameter of roughly 1.4 million kilometers, yet my spirit hand could almost contain it. And while size does not necessarily make sense in the spirit world, I couldn't help but consider the relative size of my complete soul to the relative size of a physical star. Jasmine's announcement to Douglas helped me consider the enormity of a soul. It also triggered my ego which fought against the way I was losing myself in my wonderment.

"You know," Jasmine said. "She's funny. She didn't know where the Pleiades were, but the only constellation she can pick out in the sky—the only one—is where the Pleiades is."

"Huh. What a coincidence," Douglas said.

"Hm. She's not good with messages," Jasmine said to tease me, to remind me that I was still incarnated on the earth plane. Jasmine had given me enough signs and signals throughout my life to help me find my soul base. I never paid attention, however. At least, not fully.

"Why do I get different versions of the future?" Douglas asked.

"Oh, because there are different versions of the future," Jasmine replied immediately. "The energy has shifted a little—just a little—so the version of the future that you now are on path to is slightly different than it was last week in earth time," she explained. "And that's the goal of all the messages that are being transmitted. Little by little, we changed that energy. Moved it slightly. A tiny little bit until eventually it changes for the better," Jasmine explained. "It helps to save humanity. It helps to save the earth, and it protects the rest of the universes from setback."

"Am I understanding correctly that if that transition or transformation doesn't occur, there will be no new earth?" Douglas asked.

Jasmine hesitated. "Not a new earth," she said. "But there will be new planets. There are always new creations, but we have liked some of the features on earth, and so we will add them to other creations."

"Right," Douglas said and then continued. "But the earth . . . you know what I'm referring to . . . there are references are being made to the new earth basically being in the fifth dimension."

"The soul . . . the lightworkers moving to a new dimension, you mean? "Yes."

"That will happen. But that will not be as easy as you've been told. It's not just a transplanting of souls."

"You care to elaborate on that?" Douglas joked.

"I can only tell you a little; you won't understand most of it," Jasmine responded without the least bit of intention to hurt. "But your soul is not used to the dimension yet."

"Yes."

"That will be a difficult process. There will be a transfer of some souls—not all. Not all lightworkers," she added in correction. "There will be others who join. It's more of an acceptance rather than a designation of soul. The others will return to their homes, and they will spend a great deal of earth time recovering. There's been great progress. It's regrettable if that should be the case," Jasmine said of humans.

"Right."

"Humans are on the brink of becoming more dimensional, and sometimes you can feel it in your thought processes, but also in the way you see things. There's a shift in the perception field, and so it would be that such progress would end with the end of the earth," Jasmine said matter-of-factly. "Or, at least, would retreat."

"So, is there still that possibility that the Arcturians would be the mechanism for ending the earth?" Douglas asked.

"There is, of course," Jasmine said almost too gleefully; "they have free will. But they have recognized the truth—not all of them. They have recognized the truth that if they are the ones, they would bring about their own setback," Jasmine laughed at the foolishness of it. "And there's a point where they make a decision, and there still would be time for earth to change its direction."

"Mm-hmm."

"So, it's that gamble that many of the Arcturians are beginning not to want to take."

"Interesting."

"There was a moment of a sonic boom in one of the earlier messages when we stood in front of the Federation," Jasmine said, referring to The Twelve. "They were given a glimpse of what their hand in such a destiny could create for themselves. The Arcturians are good. They are strategic. They are cerebral, but they are also physical. And so, they have free will. Their path right now looks less likely of using such a devastating weapon on another planet, on another creation. But that is only their path right now," she finished.

"Daunting," Douglas said.

"Mm."

"For me as a human," Douglas laughed. "Like *oh! Great!*"

"Yes. It should be," Jasmine asserted. "You're torn because you like the Arcturians side of view."

"Nahh. . . okay," Douglas agreed.

"And you like the weapon. You like the power of being in control, of determining destiny," she said.

"Mm-hmm."

"The problem is when you make that choice, you've affected your own destiny."

"Mm-hmm. I get that," Douglas said. "Do we have any time left or do we have to wrap up?"

"No. You can ask another."

"Can you speak in more detail of the darkness being drawn to the joy."

"Mm-hmm."

"You talked about the Astrals being drawn to the lightworkers."

"Mm-hmm."

"What's going on there?" Douglas asked. "Can you give me the dynamics? Help me understand the story here?"

"Do you like to laugh?"

"Sometimes," Douglas answered.

"Do you like to be involved in a group that is having a good time?"

"Yes."

"It's that attraction," Jasmine said. So, when you don't have that in your physical existence—when you don't experience joy—and then you see beings experiencing joy, you are drawn to that. But, at first, you are drawn to it as something not natural. *How could this be?* you ask yourself. And you cast even the emanation of joy as the *other*, and at first, you might seek to destroy the joy of others," Jasmine chuckled at the absurdity. "And sometimes physical beings are successful at doing this, but the more proximity you have to joy, the more joy affects who you are. You talk about the Astrals affecting DNA. The joy vibration can affect the DNA of an Astral," she explained. "Who wouldn't want to be joyful?" she asked. "Who wouldn't want mercy? Who wouldn't want beauty? And, after being drawn to it and resisting it at first–casting it as the *other*—if an Astral stays in close proximity, he will be accepted into the joy vibration. And he or she will accept it."

"Hmm. And then the story changes?" Douglas asked.

"And then the story changes," Jasmine repeated. "Yes. Yes."

"Your framework worked," Douglas chuckled

"Yes. The framework will change. The closer you are—the close the proximity—the closer you are to the vibrations, the more you are changed at the soul level. And the soul level remembers the past, its foundation, and from there, the physical entity can change as well."

"Okay," Douglas showed his understanding. "And so that's why the book?"

"Yes. The book is just one piece."

"Oh no! I got that."

"But inside, the words themselves will be the joy vibration. *Inside* the words," Jasmine articulated.

"So, it's almost not the content?"

"The content is important for cerebral people," Jasmine said. "They will always challenge the feeling. You see?"

"Mm-hmm."

"It works on many levels," Jasmine said.

"Right."

"So, your resistance to this message might be won over by a cerebral argument," she told Douglas."

"Right. I get that," he said.

"But the words themselves if read or heard will resonate joy. It's a way to *remind* each individual human of his or her natural state."

"Mm-hmm."

"I think you have time for one more, and she is fading on me."

"Okay. You know . . . I mean . . . those are the main ones I had for today honestly. I'm a little jumbled to be able to articulate clearly something in the moment."

"That's fine. She wants so much to tell you about the library," Jasmine told Douglas. "She is not allowed."

"The library? You mean where all the memories are?" Douglas asked.

"Yes. The Akashic Records."

"Yes."

"Yes, it is an interesting place."

"I bet," Douglas said. "I figured it had to be pretty interesting if the guardians are in charge of it."

"It's multi-modal, so unlike a library you understand here at the earth level, it mimics the life and the experiences and the knowledge. It's alive. It's not static."

"I got it. So, you're literally reading experiences."

"Yes!" Jasmine said excitedly.

"Yes."

"Yes. And it's," Jasmine said and stopped. "Yes, I can say this. It's not simply a memory that you're interacting with artificially; it is a memory that you are truly interacting with."

"Mm-hmm."

"But that's all she can tell you."

"That's okay. All right. Well, thank you."

"Yes."

"I will line up more questions next time."

"You did well."

"Thank you," Douglas said.

And Jasmine went silent.

As Douglas waited for my return, I spent time in a purifying process. This is the way after each visit. On this particular trip, the archangels gathered around me in a tight group, their vibrations merged so that I had the protection of all their individual vibrations. While I clearly felt mercy, peace, joy, humility, beauty, some others I couldn't distinguish. Two of the vibrations, in fact, have no translation here on earth; I accepted them anyway, of course. Combined, Divine White Light showered me, and I felt the pinging of energy throughout my body. The electric-like currents of spirit touches lifted my hair as they breezed through; goose bumps tingled on my skin. It is hard to leave such connection, but the always efficient Archangel Michael nodded at me when it was time to return. Although the climb to the door that *leads* to my sacred space is always memorable, always a celebration, I rarely remember the return trip. Except for the moment when the door reappears.

It is time, Michael nodded to the newly materialized door. After so many experiences, I know better than to try and negotiate a longer stay. It won't happen, so I shake my head in consent and find myself instantaneously in Douglas's office.

"You can't imagine what they see," I said when I return; "I don't want to forget."

Except for a few really cool, cosmic images, unfortunately, I *have* forgotten. I can feel the heartbeat of The Twelve—not as strong—but strong enough to remember the sensation of individual souls connected on a grid at the heart of their core. I remember the feeling of near limitlessness as my soul-self reached out to touch stars, and I remember the voices of the dispossessed souls on the earth. We—earth beings, I mean—are so much better than we appear. We have been chosen to radiate joy through the earth and out into the universes. *We have been chosen.* At heart, we are playful, trusting, loving, full of mischief and fun. There are few physical beings in the universes who have this wonderful cocktail of joy, yet we squander it on hate and division.

This message is a wake-up call for us to rediscover what we already know at our core soul level. It is a chance for us to redirect our passions towards a path that will not only save us and our world but also increase the joy and advancement of other physical beings throughout the universes. We have been created with a particular mission in mind, and before we squander our inheritance by continuing to forego this mission, we need to wake up to a life of love and joy. It is not a hard choice. We are being asked to give up hate and division for something so much better. We are being asked to come home to ourselves, to what resonates for us on the soul level.

And that long-haired, hippie-type poet? Well, he had it going on as far as messages go:

> *Nothing you can make that can't be made*
> *No one you can save that can't be saved*
> *Nothing you can do, but you can learn how to be you in time*
> *It's easy*
> *All you need is love.*

Yup. All we need is love.

ACT VII

The Source of All Things

9 July 2019

*There are times when a feeling of expectancy comes to me, as
if something is there, beneath the surface of my understanding,
waiting for me to grasp it. It is the same tantalizing sensation
when you almost remember a name, but don't quite reach it.*

~Sylvia Plath

Ethel from Decatur and Other Important Reminders

Something there is that doesn't love a wall,

That wants it down.

~Robert Frost

Hours after the seventh session with Douglas, I sat at my desk teaching a student. We were face-to-face, she on one end of a computer screen, me on the other. But she could not hear me or, more importantly, she could not understand my words without an intermediary. She is deaf; English as a spoken language is a foreign language to her. Since I only know basic, Kindergarten-level sign language, neither of us spoke the other's native language well enough to truly communicate. The student had an interpreter to relay her messages to me, so I could understand, and in turn, the interpreter relayed my messages to her. The interpreter, then, spoke both our native languages well enough to aid in our communication. The interaction seemed to be illustrative of the communication between The Twelve and humanity. We humans had forgotten the native language of the soul, and we needed an interpreter. I have become that interpreter, the intermediary of the message, the go-between.

Over the course of my sessions with Douglas, I have come to believe—well almost—what I could not accept at the beginning. The talk of ascended masters, the long-held disagreement between the Stellars and the Astrals, the Astrals' hold on humanity, and humanity's own hand in their imminent annihilation seemed the discourse of the implausible. Over the weeks—and it has only been seven weeks—I learned the implausible made intuitive sense. We humans are living our everyday lives without a recognition of the danger we face.

As I taught last Tuesday afternoon, I looked out over my laptop to see a few police in riot gear carrying guns in the quiet quad between townhouses. It did not occur to me that I was in danger; after all, I live in a safe place. Or, at least, that's what I have been told. The day was beautiful; layered white clouds hung suspended in a beautiful blue sky. The neighbor with the yellow old-fashioned-looking lawn furniture and the sleek red grill had her little black and white and gray shitzu out on the green grass, browned a bit by the recent mowing. Off in the distance, the permanence of the still snow-capped Rocky Mountains in July framed the scene from my window. All was well with the world. Except that it wasn't.

As I talked and the interpreter signed, more and more police in riot gear showed up in the bucolic setting where I live. A glimpse of the parking lot to the left of my building showed a bevy of armored vehicles and white cop cars. An email from the homeowner's association tried to blast through my inability to see what was transpiring right in front of my eyes.

Dear Resident

There is an armed individual that has barricaded themselves in an apartment home on the property and the police are currently on site. We have been instructed by the police that all residents MUST STAY inside their apartment home, and if you are not currently at the community, please do not return.

I skimmed the email with only a fragment of my full attention; the rest remained with my student. While I may not have been convinced of the danger, I was keenly aware of the grammatical errors in the message. An English teach thing, I guess. And when the police began banging on my door, I ignored it at first; I was teaching. I looked at the clock on my computer. I would be finished the class in four minutes; then, I would answer. The banging grew louder: *thump, thump, thump, thump, thump*. The police began to yell "Open up!"

"I'm sorry," I said to the interpreter; "there are police at my door," I explained and waited for her to sign and for my student to respond. "I have to go," I said finally, closing the computer link between us.

When I answered the door, the SWAT team member asked me how many people were in the apartment, "Only me and my dog," I answered.

"You have twenty seconds to get the dog and get out!" he barked. "There is an active shooter in the apartment behind you!"

"Okay," I said much too calmly. "May I take my computer?"

He rolled his eyes, "Get it," he yelled; "you have twenty seconds."

By now the parking lot was filled with armored vehicles and squad cars. The quad in front of my townhome held a corps of big gun-carrying cops in full body armor. I still did not adequately calculate the danger despite the fact that it was playing in front of my own eyes.

Dog on leash, computer in hand, wallet and phone in my pocket, I finally left the apartment to a melee of drama. Cops shouting on walkie-talkies had descended on my community. Residents ran to their cars and looked apprehensively around them as they hit the open of the parking lot. Kids screamed. An old woman with a walker stood in the middle of it all, crying, lost, bewildered.

"Hi. I'm Jackie," I said. "I'll take care of you. Get in the car."

Despite the active shooter, I calmly took the woman's arm, guided her to the front seat of the car, returned for the walker, folded it, rearranged the trunk so it would fit, and finally got in the car to start the engine. As we made our way to the gate of the community, the woman started to cry. She had left the pork chops on in the oven. I stopped to talk to the policeman.

"My friend," I said leaning out the window, "has left her pork chops on in the oven."

I looked to my new friend.

"C112," she said.

"C112," I told the cop.

"I'll take care of it," he reassured me; "have a good day," he said.

"Whaaat?" I said and started laughing.

"Have a good *rest* of the day," he corrected himself.

Because I could not make this up, I took my new friend, Ethel from Decatur, to an out-door restaurant that allowed dogs. We had a lovely afternoon sipping iced tea and telling stories. When we received the all-clear, we drove back to our townhouses and resumed our lives.

Only later, did it occur to me that I had been in real danger. I could see it playing out in front of me, but I could not accept the truth of it. Despite the more than fifty police officers, many of them in riot gear, the armored vehicles pulled up and around my block of townhomes, and the pants-on-fire warning of the email from the main office, I assumed everything would be all right and I would go on with my life as it always was. And even though that is precisely what happened, it could have been a very different story. A story I had not considered possible because I was too blind to heed all the warnings. And there were a lot of warnings.

After I received the session's recording from Douglas, I reached out to tell him the story of the shooter and the cops and Ethel from Decatur. He sent back a reply:

> *Not sure why these incidents are happening, maybe in part to show you how protected you are. AA Michael is a formidable being and I suspect he's not the only one protecting you. I am glad it ended peacefully (so Arcturian of him!) and you weren't harmed!*

While I am grateful for the protection, I now believe the incident was to show me just how blind we humans are to the myriad signs that have been sent our way to help move us from the path we are on. Regardless of the strength of these signs—natural disasters, the burning of Notre Dame in the spring, clear indications of hate and division all around us—we pacify ourselves with the everyday trivial to keep us from recognizing the truth. We—humans and our beautiful planet—are on a collision course with destiny. We are in trouble. Yet hope abounds. We can avert our ending by recognizing the logic of the message that is being shared with us. When we disavow hate and division, we can experience the joy vibration in our lives in an exponentially bigger collective way. We can take back our mission and the happiness that goes with it. And so, I believe in the signs that are playing out right in front of my eyes and the intuitive good sense of the message I have heard.

The Seventh Hypnotic Session: The History of the Universe and Other Really Cool Things

"You're at that door to your sacred space," Douglas said. "Go ahead. Open it. Step through. Close it behind you and move into your sacred space."

Once I entered through the suspended door, there was, as always, overwhelming radiance, a swarm of spirit touches, layered thoughts and feelings and the memories of all coming at me at the same time. On the entrance into my sacred space, time ended and simultaneity began. For the first few moments of earth time, I experienced chaos while Douglas heard silence. My adjustment was slow. *It's a matter of remembering*, the archangel Michael reminded me.

"There was a lot of spirit who pushed through to this dimension," I told Douglas, referring to the spirit that met me on the climb to my sacred space. "Because they could," I laughed at their explanation. "There was a crowd here before the count to the sacred space," I said gesturing to Douglas's office.

As I spoke, my voice was distant, almost hazy. I was busy watching the archangels arrange themselves in front of The Twelve, and I was keenly aware of the emanation of Source, its pulsating, energizing vitality pulling, pulling, pulling me towards it. Always. Not unexpectedly then, my full attention was not completely on narrating the experiences with the spirit on the climb to my sacred space.

"And that was kind of ruckus and funny," I said of the spirit. "And it wasn't like normal spirit touches. They were kind of bumping and knocking me around, and everybody was trying to get up the steps at the same time. And when I opened the door, I pushed through first and spilled out to the same place I was the last time session," I laughed. "And even Archangel Michael is more relaxed," I noted. "He wasn't . . . not *angry* . . . but not as efficient as normal, and he allowed the spirits to just bound up the stairs with us, I guess. That's the way they were acting. But there were more archangels with us today," I said. "I don't know if this is from the *Little Mermaid*, but I heard *Ariel*."

"Mm-hmm," Douglas said.

"I think she's an angel."

"Yes," Douglas acknowledged.

"I think she's an archangel."

"Yes, she is," he confirmed.

"She's pink. She radiates pink. And the smoky one was with us. Like Ra . . . like Rag . . . like Ragwell," I tried to get the name correct. "Like Rag . . .".

"Raguel," Douglas said.

"Raguel," I repeated, trying out the sound.

"And there was one that was like a chocolate brown color," I giggled, "and I thought that was unfortunate as a color against the cotton candy colors of the others, but he thought chocolate was better than cotton candy any day," I laughed.

As I discussed the colors of archangels, I realized—although somewhere I already knew this, had always known this—the colors of the archangels represented their main vibrations. Archangels can vibrate all vibrations, and they can vibrate the merging of all vibrations in the form of the Divine White Light of love and protection. But they all have specific jobs and focus more particularly on the vibration that helps them complete them.

Archangel Michael, for example, mostly radiates a deep, dark purple which connotes strength through compassion. At times, Michael also vibrates the Divine White Light, the crystalline nature of which always appears within his purple radiance. Archangel Raphael vibrates the deep green of healing that radiates most with the human heart, and Archangel Gabriel vibrates the pretty light blue of communication that radiates most with the human throat.

"I don't know who . . . maybe a Z," I said referring to first letter of the brown archangel's name.

"Zadkiel?" Douglas asked.

I tried out the name in my mind several times, turning it over and over before responding, 'Zad . . . Zadkiel?"

"Mm-hmm," Douglas answered.

"Zadkiel," I whispered and waited for guidance that I never got. "But they're all here," I said moving on. "As soon as we opened the door, they took their place. The pink was mostly," I stopped and corrected, "the *Little Mermaid* one, she was most interested in me. She leaned in several times and touched me," I said. "I think she finds the elasticity of my skin funny," I said. "I think I've seen her before; she's the one," I laughed. "She's the one that kind of reminds me of the doughty British woman."

"Mm," Douglas said.

Although I had seen the pink archangel before—Ariel, she had a more regal appearance in this manifestation. Her light stood tall, erect, more majestic. In past hypnotic sessions, she had been shorter and wider.

"Raphael has a special role in today's *services*," I said unsure of the word; "that's what I heard them call it. He is deep green; it's pretty. It's almost like emerald, and he almost looks like a long, elongated diamond shape in the way he's radiating today," I said as if the description was normal.

It wasn't long until The Twelve called my attention away from the archangels. While I had already seen them in my peripheral vision, looking at them full on was always a surprise. They were spectacular in the colors and harmonics that I cannot describe with my limited earth vocabulary. Like lifting my face to the sun, eyes closed, I was met with the warmth of their vibrations pouring not just over me, but through me and around me and in me. It filled every space of my almost infinite soul. Although I felt overwhelming, incomprehensible love from the combined effect, I could also feel each of their separate emanations.

"The Twelve have a mission today," I said and began to whisper so quietly that what I said was not distinguishable on the recording; I was physically speaking to the non-incarnated spirit presence of The Twelve. "It's almost hard to breathe," I whispered and spent the next minute forcing myself to breathe in and out in Douglas's office. "Source is," I said and stopped to find the words to express what I saw. "Too hard to explain, but I'm just going to let the words fall out and, then, make sense of them later."

"Okay."

"Source is," I tried and stopped again. "How I look at the scenery is through earth eyes, and I see the archangels in an arc in front of me, almost as if they're protecting me. And then there are *so* many souls, *so* many souls," I repeated. "Behind the archangels, it almost looks like mountains of soul. And, then, raised just a bit higher is The Twelve, but they're really not on anything. And then behind them is Source, but that's just how I see it. It's more like," I stopped for guidance. "Like a snow globe. You know?" I finally blurted out. "Like Source is the outside of the snow globe, and inside is everything else, and except that you can see it best," I tried to explain. "You can see Source best in the far panel of the snow globe, but it's really the whole snow globe. The whole thing," I finished excitedly.

"Mm-hmm," Douglas said.

"And The Twelve laugh because Source is there all the time," I laughed in return. "And only sometimes I notice it."

"Yeah," Douglas said in a long, understanding drawl.

"And when I do, it's so overpowering," I said, ignoring Douglas, trying to explain the unexplainable. "It's hard to breathe," I said and stopped for a long silence in awe. "It's this magnificent creative force. It's energy, but it's a buzzing. It's a buzz. That's the best way to say it," the description spilled out of me. "It's a buzz. And it looks like an eclipse of the sun," I said, "where it's black in the middle, and the aura—the light—comes out all the way around it. And it's like that because it's so bright we," I stopped to regroup. "It's so bright, I can't see it. The middle becomes black to me because it's so bright," I said. "And The Twelve are calling me forward again. Phew," I breathed out with the change of focus.

When my soul noticed and stood within the majesty of Source, I had the deep need to remain in front of it. I could stay, living in the pure bliss, absolute love, infinitude of Source for eternity. And I would be happy. Nothing else mattered. Nothing else could. My soul resonated as it should; to redirect my gaze, then, to *anything* else was a monumental task. The Twelve, however, were very persuasive.

"And I want to do this, but I know what it feels like now," I said as The Twelve—Jasmine in particular—summoned me to them. "And so I'm a little scared."

"Hm," Douglas signaled his understanding.

"Last time I didn't know what it felt like."

"Michael can take your fear if you like," Douglas said.

"Michael's so far back," I said and laughed. "Well, not anymore," I corrected myself as he stood by my side.

"Right."

"He took my hand to them," I said as Michael led me to The Twelve. "Like a child. I feel like a child. After a long silence in which I accepted the invitation of The Twelve, I told Douglas, "and there are the images. They're not images," I corrected myself; "they're real, and I see things in . . . um . . . you know what film does. . . I think it's called *time release*? . . . where they film over hours and, then, you see it all in fifteen seconds?"

"Right."

"That's what I'm seeing except that's just the way time is here. There is no time," I explained. "Oh, I can see the mountains, and I can see the sunset and the sunrise almost simultaneously.

As I noticed the images The Twelve experienced regularly, I noticed the library where the Akashic records were kept. The records held the history of creation, not just the past, but the future as well although such terms do not actually exist on the spirit plane. I saw the library as a Grecian temple: high white Grecian pillars—Doric, they were—spanning the clean lines of an open-air, white marbled foyer. Inside an eternity of books filled the space. There were no shelves. In fact, the only physical structure was the temple itself.

Just walking through the threshold, I gained the knowledge of all things from every incarnation in every star system and universe. I experienced every memory of every soul who had ever incarnated anywhere. The knowledge came all at once; the impact was almost physical. Whispers of everything—every scientific treatise, every philosophical debate, every guru's wonderings, every work of literature, art, sculpture, everything from everywhere—filled the space of the Akashic records. The books were alive; their whispers almost indistinguishable in the chaos of knowledge.

Guardians filled the interior; they were a group of spirits who, as a joke, presented themselves as the ghost-like fixtures of 1940 Hollywood black-and-whites. With a simple thought from me, they chose, delivered, and opened the appropriate book; the process was instantaneous, of course, as was the accumulation of knowledge from the book. The book isolated a particular subject—a singular study—from the cacophony of whispers. There was no need to read it; I only needed to rest my hands on it, and worlds exploded from it. I lived memories and saw the great moments of physical incarnations in the universe where earth calls home. I heard the pleas and experienced the pleasure of other physical incarnations, cried for the loneliness of some of the souls in a physical existence and marveled at the creation of new life. I saw my birth, relived the birth of my children, experienced the births of my own parents. I heard the thoughts of the profound and reveled in the everyday bliss of the simple.

"Ohh! It's the history of our universe," I said. "I can explain it like this," I said referring to the creation of our universe. "Imagine that you had a balloon that was filled with air, and if you could—if it was possible, you sucked all the air out," I said as I made the sound of sucking. "You sucked all the air out. Not just *let* it out, but *sucked* all the air out. And then—*hooh*," I breathed out. "All in one shot—*hooh*—the balloon filled again. That's how . . . that's how our universe started. It was," I said making a sucking noise, "contraction, and, then—*hooh*, expansion," I explained.

As if on cue, I saw the flood that changed the physical face of the earth and the fate of earth dwellers. This was the conversation that had been hinted at in the last hypnotic session, but not fully explained. In utter dismay, I saw the cause of such destruction. It was not, as has long been asserted by scientists, an asteroid.

"Ohh!" I exclaimed. "We were highly intellectual; in fact, we were advanced, and we communicated with the Stellars. So we were Stellars. We weren't as advanced as them," I clarified, "but we lived in a denser dimension. But we had the technology to communicate," I said and then turned to address the cause. "It wasn't an asteroid, and it wasn't a meteorite. It was a weapon," I said referring to the cataclysm that hit the earth 11,000 years ago. "And the impact of it broke apart the ice caps. So many were killed; this is Noah's flood," I explained. "Winter came," I whispered after a very long silence. "And it affected the environment for three generations. One hundred years. The crops wouldn't grow, and we regressed. And after one hundred years, we forgot. In Egypt in the Valley of the Kings in the tombs, there are records of this. Yeah, I remember. I remember," I said.

As I experienced the one hundred years of devastation and starvation and watched the deterioration of a once-more advanced earth civilization into bitter, embattled tribal units, I was shown the markers, the records of the time that still remained intact on the earth. In the Valley of the Kings, my son and I stood in front of a wall of intricate, beautifully-colored paintings in an underground tomb. One image reappeared over and over again in the lines and lines of wall-painted story; it stood out from among the others, those dressed in the white-linen-ed look of the pharaonic Egyptians. The image in contrast, however, looked like a modern-day space traveler, glass-fronted helmet and all. We—my son and I—could not make sense of it. But sense was in short supply in that dimly lit, heat-heavy crypt. That any of the images could survive the dry heat and sand-blasted devastation of the surrounding location was astounding; that the images could be so beautifully wrought in colors so vibrant, so alive, so magnificent by an ancient hand was astonishing. Yet, there on the walls of a tomb in the sand-colored otherwise colorless hills of the Egyptian desert, such treasures existed to tell the story of what had been, and what had once been included an ancient spaceman.

You needed to see the evidence, Jasmine whispered to me. *You needed to believe,* she said of the many travels I was compelled to take, including the one to the Valley of the Kings. *The message resonates with you because you have seen it,* she concluded, and I agreed. Once more with Jasmine, I stood in front of the wall that held the image of the galactic traveler. I leaned in over the metal bar that separated me from it, and breathed in the stale arid hot of the desert tomb as I tried to make sense of what I saw.

"We feared the Stellars and closed ourselves off," I began to tell the story of earth after the devastation. "And that's when our story really became entangled with the Astral's. We were easy marks then," I said. "Many of the ancients had access to the Stellar technology. We accepted their help. We didn't travel to them, but they traveled to us," I explained. "We weren't able yet to travel to them," I said. "But that all changed," I sighed sadly. "Some Stellars refused to leave the earth, and some were stuck here. Enough that our DNA is made from the stuff of stars," I said. "That is our history," I summed up.

Although I stood in the library temple of the Akashic records, I also stood in front of the paintings of the tomb in the Valley of the Kings. *There are others,* Jasmine whispered to me, reminding me of additional unexplainable things I had seen in my travels. I looked up at her for explanation. *In time,* she said. *When it's right.*

"There's a saying *as above, so below.* I heard it many . . . many times in my life, but I couldn't quite get it," I admitted. "But at every level, I see the same. The Twelve link in vibration. The archangels link in vibration The Stellars link in vibration," I chuckled. "It's just us. Humans have forgotten," I said a little embarrassed.

Overwhelmed as I was by the paintings on the wall of the underground tomb and the knowledge in the library temple that held the Akashic records, Jasmine stepped in to relay the message.

A Message from The Twelve: Accepting that We are Holograms of Source

"While she explores, you can ask questions," Jasmine said to Douglas.

"What was . . .," Douglas stopped to clear his throat; "what was the purpose and the utilization of the weapon?"

"Enslavement," was Jasmine's simple complex answer. "But it marked the others as well. The users were caught in the vibration," she said meaning those who had fired the weapon. "And so while it worked on some level, it regressed the civilizations," she said. "They couldn't remember why they used it either," she chuckled at the absurdity of it all. "There was a sense, however, a rationale put forward that it would restart or reboot the earth civilization. Those that used it did not realize that it would ripple out and affect them as well, and it did reboot, but to a much more primitive state than even earthlings were created in."

"What had they hoped would occur with the use of this weapon?" Douglas asked. "What was the intention?"

"The intention was to change the effects of the DNA manipulation. They thought it was strategic, but they did not know the power it would have on the creation. And it wasn't a strategic shot; it was devastating. Knowledge was lost. Peoples were lost. Know-how was lost," she said sadly. "When the weapon was used, they thought it was surgical; they did not know the power of it. And it was the Stellars," Jasmine announced. "And they tried to help; they knew what they had done. And they tried to help, but by then, the beings on earth had become so primitive, they had become distrustful. At first, they accepted them as gods. The Stellars," Jasmine laughed. "And the Stellars played along because they thought it was for the greater good, it would be a way to help. But their vanity got in the way."

"I'm sorry; what got in the way?" Douglas asked.

"Their vanity."

"The Stellar's vanity?" Douglas asked for clarification.

"Yes."

"Yeah," he said.

"They enjoyed the fealty of the earth beings, and after a while, they forgot that they were there to help. Those that stayed, however, also became primitive in their ways. They took on and accepted the limits of the earth space."

"So they forgot?" Douglas asked.

"They forgot. They just thought they were special. They thought they were endowed by the Heavens, and they forgot that they were *from* the Heavens. They were a physical being—a soul incarnated in a physical body; the same as the earth beings," she said. "It's proximity," Jasmine explained. "Your DNA changes to the vibration that you are so close to."

"You used the word *enslavement* earlier," Douglas began.

"Yes."

"Was the intention to perpetuate the enslavement with the use of the weapon?" he asked; "or to decrease the . . .".

"To end it."

"To end the enslavement, right?" Douglas asked.

"Yes," Jasmine answered.

"Okay, I just wanted to make sure I got it straight," Douglas said. "So they thought that it would be beneficial?"

"Yes."

"Okay."

226

"Yes," Jasmine repeated. "The intent was good," she chuckled.

"And was this . . . was this done by the Arcturians?" Douglas asked.

"Yes. And by others."

"Mm-hmm," Douglas agreed.

"The Arcturians have forgotten that history, and they've been reminded recently."

"How are they doing with that?" Douglas asked a little sarcastically.

"As you might expect," Jasmine chuckled. "But they have also recognized that the Astrals are they. We are *all* holograms of Source. We are all the *same* at our essence."

Jasmine set another book from the Akashic records before me. I experienced the creation of the universes, of time, of souls. I saw the emergence of emanations from Source: creation at its purest. And although I can no longer recall it, I understood the reason why we were created and why we choose physical expressions from time to time. I knew. I saw. I experienced it all.

"Think how foolish it is for one to hate another because of a physical characteristic," Jasmine instructed Douglas. "How foolish! What makes one physical characteristic different? And then what makes one physical characteristic better?" Jasmine asked. "It's illogical. The leap is illogical," she emphasized. "And the only thing that can account for it is hate, division," Jasmine explained. "It's easy to find a physical characteristic; you can see it. You can sense it in the earth realm, and therefore you can categorize it as the *other*," she said.

After a significant silence, Douglas asked, "So am I to understand that the Stellars who stayed became the Astrals?"

"Umm . . . some," Jasmine said, hesitating just a bit in her answer. "Some of those who used the weapon were cast out of the group. Not all Arcturians. Some Arcturians. And others," she clarified. "And they became branded as the *other*," she explained. "It's the *Cain and Abel* story of the Stellars, but the Stellars forgot the origin of the Astrals. They have maintained the feud. For millennia," she announced. "Two houses both alike," Jasmine chuckled; "two houses both alike in dignity," she said referring to the opening lines of Shakespeare's *Romeo and Juliet.*

"And deep-seated in the Arcturian soul is the idea that the Astrals affect the Arcturian mission of peace. It's like a little trace," Jasmine clarified, "a little bit of memory that's left over . . . that's left in their DNA," she said. "And so they continue to fight with the Astrals," she said of the Stellars, "rather than invite them home. I'm not saying it would be easy," Jasmine conceded. "They're physical beings, but I believe over millennia had that been the opportunity for the Astrals, things would have been different today."

"Do the Astrals know their history?" Douglas asked. "Their origins?"

"Some. Not many," Jasmine responded. "Remember the use of the weapon backfired, affected them as well. While they certainly didn't regress as much as the earth inhabitants regressed, they regressed enough so there is only a trace of memory left in them. They have no *context* for the trace of memory, only that trace of memory," she explained. "And so they think they are fighting with the Arcturians," she laughed "because the Arcturians don't accept their way of life. And yet they don't know their soul base is Arcturian. And others," she clarified. "It's what happens when memory gets divorced from context," Jasmine explained. "It happens in humanity as well. That's what Shakespeare wrote about in *Romeo and Juliet*," she said. "A feud divorced from context. Nobody remembered why they fought—the two houses. They just remembered to fight."

At the first mention of arguably Shakespeare's most famous play, Jasmine transported me to the premiere of the play in Elizabethan England. Although an English professor should have been delighted by a first-hand introduction to the work of the bard, the first thing I noticed was neither the play nor the actors. I didn't immediately notice the carved wooden structure that sat above the stage or the crowd packed shoulder to shoulder on the floor of the not very ornate theatre. Instead, a wall of stinking, sweaty, oily stench hit me like a tidal wave, and Jasmine laughed at my visceral reaction.

Turn it off, she told me, but I didn't know how to deaden the sense of smell. *I always hated teaching this play,* I played with Jasmine.

"She hates that play, she tells me," Jasmine said recounting our experience at *The Globe* for Douglas. Jasmine laughed.

"I'm sorry; what play?" Douglas asked.

"She hates *Romeo and Juliet* actually," Jasmine continued to laugh.

"Oh. Yeah," Douglas said.

"But it illustrates the point," Jasmine explained.

"I got that," Douglas said. "So there's really basically a feud going on between the Astrals and the Stellars?" Douglas asked.

"Yes."

"Well, that puts a few things in context."

"Yes. Foolish, isn't it?" Jasmine asked.

"Yeees," Douglas drawled. "But then so were the two houses that fought in *Romeo and Juliet* and . . .".

"Yes. Yes," Jasmine whispered.

"And when you hold on it to that degree, you fight til the death," Douglas explained.

"Yes, and you lose the context," she laughed.

"Right."

"The historical perspective is gone; only the fight remains. The fight not connected or contracted to any historical event loses any means of being resolved," Jasmine warned.

"Hm," Douglas agreed. After a long silence, he asked, "So the Astrals would like to fight the Stellars?"

"Hmm . . . fight in terms of not necessarily in a military battle, as you might think. But *resist* is maybe a good way of saying it. Resist their way of life. Resist their understanding of the world. Resist the peace vibration. Resist it all," Jasmine explained. "And in that way, continue the feud. Does that make sense?"

"I think so," Douglas answered.

"To resist another's way of thought, another's opinion, another's way of looking at the world or worlds is as aggressive as fighting. You cannot come to any agreement if you refuse to engage. And now the Stellars are seeing this," she conceded. "It will take more time than it should in earth years for it to resolve itself, but they're on the path. Most," she clarified. "And now we have earth in the middle of the feud."

"Hm," Douglas interjected. "You read my mind."

"It is a specialty," Jasmine joked.

"Yeah," Douglas laughed. "And suddenly it's like *Oh!* And here's humanity on the brink in the middle."

"Yes," Jasmine whispered calmly.

"Yay!" Douglas joked.

"Humanity is not without sin here though," Jasmine counseled. "And I don't mean sin in a religious sense. They have had a part in their own subjugation. They have accepted the story, and they have accepted *hate* into their hearts. They *are* part of the problem. It is illogical for them not to accept joy in order to have hate," she explained, "It is illogical, but it is part of their story," she conceded recognizing the role of free will in humanity's current crisis. "Or their framework," Jasmine added for Douglas. "Those on earth have begun to see themselves in reference to others. They are who they are because they are not like the *other*," Jasmine explained the story that humanity believes. "And they have forgotten the fundamental truth," she chuckled, "that we are holograms of Source. We are *all* the same. And even in a very basic human sense, we are all the same. The animal body is made up of a network of veins, a heart, a brain, kidneys. It functions and acts and stops functioning in the same way for everyone," she forcefully pointed out.

"There is no difference at the physical level either, and yet the physical characteristic," Jasmine laughed, "the most superficial, the *least* important part of a human being is used to cast the *other*. Why brown skin and not brown eyes?" she asked. "What makes skin color more important than eye color? Why brown skin and not brown hair?" she asked to illustrate the lack of logic. "What makes skin color more important than other characteristics? Why language?" she asked. "Why language, a form of communication? Why religion? Why religion, a form of recognizing Source? Why? It's illogical, and in choosing the superficial to categorize, joy is lost," she warned. "Except on the basic, fundamental, individual, every day level," she explained. "Humans must expand what they experience at the individual level to the community level and eventually to the world level," Jasmine instructed.

As she spoke, I witnessed the transformation that would come if we survived, if we expanded the joy we experienced at the individual level. We would move to a new dimension. Like moving from black-and-white photographs to colored ones or from the stereopticon images at the beginning of *The Wizard of Oz* to the dramatic Technicolor screen as Dorothy opens the door to Oz, our ability to perceive will explode, expanding our senses and opening our understanding exponentially.

"There is a renaissance about to occur for humanity. You feel it," Jasmine told Douglas. "You feel the higher being calling; others do too. You need to survive to get there," she warned. "The path has shifted," she said with a little hope. "The path has shifted and has bought you some time. In earth time," she said. "Not much," she added to clarify our predicament. "But some. You will not win everyone with this book, and no message will capture everyone. But the goal is to create and capture a critical mass, and in so doing, change the overall vibration of the earth. The Stellars are working out their part," she said after some silence. "The Astrals will too, but humans must have a part in saving themselves."

In the long silence between the last part of Jasmine's question and the next, I was shown one potential path of my own future. Although it sounds hokey, I saw an older me with a golden brown-haired little girl, a clip pulling a wisp of hair across her forehead to the right. Her eyes reflected the color of Archangel Raphael in their deep emerald shine. A little shift of a dress, sleeveless, pale colors with tiny flowers, covered her pale-white, baby-fatted arms. White puffs from the cottonwood trees floated in the late-spring air, and the cerulean blue of the sky seemed gloriously close to the new green of the grass as I held my arms out to the tottering toddler who recognized me as a soul mate.

"We are showing her success in the alternate path," Jasmine said referring to me. "She will have a granddaughter with a small piece of her greater soul, and they will be inseparable," Jasmine said emphasizing *they will be inseparable*. "And she will work for it," she said referring to my desire to have such a future. "You will have one more question?" Jasmine asked Douglas.

"Let's talk about mission if we might," Douglas said.

"Yes."

"It's an important word."

"Yes."

"And yet, as it is," Douglas began, "as it is typical with those kinds of words, the more you move towards it, the further . . . it becomes elusive," Douglas explained.

"And the more you define it," Jasmine broke in, "the more rigid and inaccessible it becomes."

"Okay. It feels intuitively correct," Douglas conceded. "Can you put more words to why that is? Help me with . . . I'm trying to," Douglas said struggling with the phrasing; "part of it is I've got to be able to write to it . . .".

"Yes," Jasmine whispered.

"And I'm having trouble with capturing what exactly it is," Douglas continued; "do we have a lot of different missions?"

"Yes," Jasmine said emphatically. "Mission is not one thing; mission is many things. Mission is many things," she reiterated for emphasis. "And you will complete missions. You *have* completed missions," she assured Douglas. "There is a great soul contract that you have . . . a personal soul contract, and it's something that you've come to learn in this physical incarnation. For you, we've identified it. It's confidence. For her," she said referring to me, "it's forgiveness. There is a collective contract that you sign with a soul group," she added, "and that's for the greater good of, in this case, humanity. But more than just humanity," she elaborated. "The Stellars. The Astrals. The other universes," she expanded the effect to those affected by the greater good. "Your success in that collective contract will be good for all universes," Jasmine declared. "Sometimes they compete—the missions at the personal level with the bigger mission," she said. "Self-sacrifice is often required at the soul contract level—the collective contract," she explained. "And that is not in keeping with the personal contract. Do you see?" she asked Douglas.

"Abstractly, I do," he admitted.

Yes. And it will be abstract," Jasmine conceded. "Your goal in a personal contract is to live through an entire life in order to gain the lessons, but on occasion when you choose self-sacrifice for a collective contract, you have relinquished some of that personal contract. As she does with the message," Jasmine said, reminding Douglas of the contract with The Twelve in which I agreed to fewer earth years. "And because they compete from time to time, you feel that urge to fold up and not complete either. But that, too, is part of the mission," she confided. "If it were easy, it would not be a worthy lesson. And remember as you make soul contracts, in general, but not always," she said, "you are at the soul level. A full, complete soul making contracts. Only a small piece of that soul inhabits a physical body," she explained, "and that's why you forget it, and the physical body can also interfere in you finding your mission. In a sense-rich environment like earth, there are competing interests. Have I helped at all?" Jasmine asked Douglas.

"Yes. Is there a specific mission that goes with being part of humanity?" he asked.

"Yes. To vibrate joy," she said with great energy.

"So that's the understanding of any soul who incarnates on this planet?" Douglas asked.

"Yes. And that will be particularly difficult for those with a soul foundation in a different native vibration," Jasmine explained. "So if your soul foundation is Arcturian," she illustrated, "and they vibrate peace, and you come into a new existence to vibrate joy, it feels uncomfortable to you. But it is something you need to learn. There is a reason," she explained. "If you learn to vibrate all, you can vibrate Divine White Light. It is worthy," she finished.

"So then the choice of the first incarnation—wherever that is—is incredibly important because that soul is going to be imprinted with that vibration?" Douglas asked.

"Mm," Jasmine interrupted, showing her appreciation of the word *imprinted*. "Imprinted is a very good word for it. Not *stuck* in it," she explained referring to the soul foundation, "imprinted is much better. I've talked about memories that have lost their historical context?"

"Mm-hmm," Douglas showed his understanding.

"So it is for souls. You are imprinted," she reiterated, almost trying out the feel of the word. "Yes. I like this word."

"That's by a soul's choice?" Douglas asked.

"Yes."

"I assume it's a very big decision for them?"

"It is, and it's because it *resonates* with you at the soul level. So she chose Pleiadean as her soul base," Jasmine used me as an illustration of her main point, "because it radiated for her. It resonated in her deepest, deepest part of her soul. She felt it, and she chose this as her first incarnation. But it's not a difficult incarnation," Jasmine said referring to my present incarnation. "Not as difficult for her to be on an earth vibration," she explained, "since it is also joy. They both vibrate joy," Jasmine said about the Pleiades and earth.

"Right," Douglas vocalized his understanding.

"She is out of step because she is *not* human at the core of her soul," Jasmine laughed. "It is not imprinted there, and so she doesn't have the instinct. Let's use an earth word," Jasmine said. "An *instinct* of earth. So your first imprint provides your instinct. Although that is an earth understanding," she admitted.

"Mm," Douglas agreed. "And yet I chose Arcturian."

"Yes."

"And yet I had all these . . . I mean, I had an incredible number of lives on this planet."

"And not this planet alone," Jasmine told Douglas. "And you very often choose mates that are different. From a different world. From a different place. From a different religion. From a different race. From a different . . ." she said. "You choose difference as part of your learning."

"Mm. At a soul level?" Douglas asked.

"At a soul level. It has made you accepting," she said as a compliment.

"Mm."

"Which is a joy vibration, so you can understand now why you have chosen many incarnations on the earth. It was a lesson you needed to learn."

"Mm," Douglas laughed. "How am I doing?"

"You have achieved. And you know this."

"Mm," he conceded.

"She is losing herself," Jasmine said of me; "she must come soon," she warned.

"Okay. Then I will . . .".

"If you have one more, you can."

"Okay," Douglas answered. "What does it mean to be an ascended master?" he asked.

"Mmmm," Jasmine drew out. "This is more abstract than any of the questions you've asked."

"Oh good," Douglas said.

"An ascended master is simply ready to reemerge with Source."

"Okay."

"You've completed your journey. It's an earth name: ascended master," Jasmine laughed.

"Yeah."

"It's not the same in the spirit world, but The Twelve have chosen to stay without merging to guide home souls. We have completed our journey. Our final step is reemerging."

"I get that," Douglas said. "So the use of the ascended masters with different physical incarnations does not match up with what you're saying?"

"You mean do we incarnate on the earth?"

"Mm-hmm."

"Yes. Yes, we do. Not often."

"And that's the point?" Douglas asked.

"Yes."

"So Buddha, I'm just picking that out, for instance," Douglas said.

"Yes," Jasmine whispered a smile at the name.

"Buddha is one of you?"

"He is *now* an ascended master," Jasmine corrected. "He was not then."

"Oh. Okay."

"It was his step," she explained.

"To be complete?" Douglas asked.

"Yes."

"Ohhh," Douglas drew out. "Okay."

"Yes, he was. He is now."

"Okay, so he is not part of The Twelve?"

"No, but he can speak through The Twelve."

"Sure."

"And his soul, you might be surprised to know, resonates female," Jasmine said.

"Hmm," Douglas considered. And after a long silence, Douglas added, "thank you."

"You are welcome," Jasmine told Douglas.

And so the message, at least for this particular book, was completed.

phenomenon, but something that must extend throughout every country—rich or poor, large or small, religious or secular.

In every major religion of the world, judgement of others is considered, at best, irreligious and, at worst, sinful. Judgement is the domain of God, the Divine, the Creator, not the domain of humans. Yet, too often members of one faith—in juxtaposition to the very foundation of their espoused beliefs—practice intolerance, bigotry, narrow-mindedness towards members of other faiths or towards members of no faith. The discourse of hate is peppered with allusions to religious doctrine, and the words of holy books or masters are manipulated to soothe the guilt that arises from the treason against core beliefs.

When we meet and speak to people who live on the other side of our arbitrary separations, we experience first-hand different ways of thinking, living, and responding to the world at large. We build empathy for others, a gift we give ourselves because, by endeavoring to understand the practices, beliefs, desires, needs, and passions of others, we can expand the ways we experience the Divine. If we practice our beliefs as the Nepalese do—without judgement and with a profound sense of love in all its manifestations—we would, I am sure, change the world into a place of kindness, compassion, respect, and tolerance.

We would link together to radiate joy.

If You Want to Live in the Light . . .

Over the course of the seven sessions, I had my eyes opened to the obvious: we humans choose hate and division over joy. It is, as Jasmine said about many of our choices, illogical. More importantly, it is *obviously* illogical. For example, there are not *others*. As Jasmine stressed over and over again, we are all the same, holograms of Source at the soul level. Even physical bodies that act as vehicles for our souls are fundamentally the same except for a few superficial physical characteristics.

So, what is it about us—humanity, I mean—that seeks out separation? Rather than honoring what we share with each other, we erect monuments—walls, borders, fences, even our words—to mark what separates us. We seek out the differences between and among us, often ignoring the feelings, characteristics, attitudes, hopes, dreams, and life circumstances that link us all together into a shared humanity. Social institutions reinforce the separation. Groups insulate themselves, and people learn to fear the *other*. Even the very vehicle that should contribute to the celebration of oneness—religious practice—often acts as a force to divide. It is clear, however, that if you want to live in the light, you cannot hold others in the dark.

Religion is the structure that allows us to practice our core spiritual beliefs and values. At the heart of most religions is a focus on love as expressed through kindness, compassion, respect, and living in harmony with each other. In the ideal, then, the *structure* of our practice—religion—should enhance the *expression* of our spiritual core, allowing us to generate love inwards to ourselves and outwards to each other and to the universes. Religion, in the ideal, would amplify a sense of shared humanity with one another even to those who practice differently. Unfortunately, the ideal is rarely realized.

But I witnessed the perfect merging of core spiritual principles and religious practices in Kathmandu, the capitol city of Nepal which sits in the shadow of Mount Everest, the birthplace of Buddha, the ascended master. The main religious practitioners—Buddhists and Hindus—view each other's choice of religious practice as destiny with a hint of free choice thrown in for good measure; they rarely consider the choice as one of right or wrong. Religious practice, they believe, is usually determined simply by being a member in a community of like-minded individuals. Live with Buddhists, in other words, and you are more likely to be a Buddhist. Live with Hindus, and . . . well, you know.

In Kathmandu, judgement is virtually non-existent, at least none is apparent, and a sense of peace and contentment infuse the people and the country. An incredibly poor country—among the poorest on the planet, in fact—the people are among the most content, the most joyous I have ever seen. Even the animals are happy, and Buddhist monks care for and feed them as lovingly as if they were pets. They are not. They are partners on this path of life, and the monks ask permission of the animals before feeding them. Even stray dogs. In the exchange, dogs sit patiently at the monks' feet, happy and excited, waiting, but doing nothing to disturb the serenity of the moment.

In Kathmandu, then, spirituality and religion work together to promote a loving and accepting practice of faith, one that extends generosity and tolerance to those who worship God, the Divine, the Creator differently. They recognize their oneness in each other and act in ways to promote connection, not division. And, I believe, this is not meant to be a singular